THE NEW OXFORD PICTURE DICTIONARY

Teacher's Guide

IRENE FRANKEL

OXFORD UNIVERSITY PRESS

Oxford University Press

198 Madison Avenue
New York, NY   10016   USA

Walton Street
Oxford OX2 6DP England

OXFORD is a trademark of Oxford University Press.

ISBN 0-19-434330-8

Senior Editor: Margot Gramer
Associate Editor: Mary Lynne Nielsen
Design Manager: Shireen Nathoo
Designer: Terry Helms

Printing (last digit): 10 9 8

Printed in the United States of America.

Contents

continued next page

Acknowledgements

I would like to express my gratitude to Margot Gramer, Senior Editor at Oxford, for her vision and expertise in the creation of this Guide. I would also like to thank Associate Editor Mary Lynne Nielsen for her meticulous attention to detail, Designer Terry Helms for her creative efforts, and Senior Editor Susan Lanzano for thinking of me in the first place.

Special thanks go to the staff of the Paterson (New Jersey) Adult Learning Center, and particularly the ESL staff—Marguerite Andre, Ralph Colognori, Glenda Harvey, and Mark Spina—for their support and encouragement.

I am grateful to many people for their help with the research for this book: Robert Martin, Rivalyn Zweig, Dr. Hal Solomon, David Martin, Richard Tremitiedi, Charles Geyer, Evan Frankel, Louis Cicchella, Royal Martin, Carol Price, Evelyn Frankel, Rochelle Buhler, Paul Hartunian, Joanne Epps, Dr. Rob Gilbert, Carole Barr, and John Featherston.

Heartfelt appreciation goes to Robert Martin for his painstaking reading of the manuscript and insightful comments and suggestions, and to David Martin for his expert technical assistance with the Apple Macintosh computer.

I am indebted to my former ESL students, especially Ofelia Hernandez, Felicita Colon, and Jean Cadena, who have enriched me both professionally and personally. I hope this book will help them and others like them master our beautiful and complex language.

Most of all, I want to thank my husband, David Martin, for all his help and support and for everything he did to make the work on this project such a joy.

Introduction

The New Oxford Picture Dictionary is a collection of pictures organized into 85 topical units, such as The Family, The Supermarket, and Public Transportation. All of the pages have lists of nouns, with the following exceptions: there are six pages of verbs, two pages of adjectives, and two pages of prepositions. The majority of the units are one page long, but some units, such as The City, are two pages.

The pictures on each page are numbered from left to right or in a clockwise pattern to facilitate picture identification. The exceptions to this are Map of the World (70–71), which is arranged by geographic items, and The United States of America (72–73), which is alphabetically arranged.

On pages where the illustrations are not contextualized, the pictures are not necessarily drawn to scale, e.g., Vegetables (6–7).

An index is provided in the back of the book, with the standard pronunciation given for each item. The pronunciation symbols used are similar to those found in first language dictionaries.

HOW TO USE A PICTURE DICTIONARY

A picture dictionary, with its clearly labeled illustrations, provides the teacher with the means to present a vocabulary item without ambiguity or the need for translation.

In learning any new lexical item, the students must be able to associate sound with meaning so that they will recognize the word upon hearing it spoken. They should be able to recognize the written item so that they will understand the word in print. The students must also be able to recall the item when they see the object itself, as well as when they wish to use it in their own speech or writing. The students' ultimate goal is to use the new vocabulary in meaningful contexts that are linguistically and culturally appropriate.

In order to help the students achieve their goal, teachers need to take the following steps:

Step 1: Present each item on a page (using the *Wall Charts*, if available), pronouncing the word while pointing to the picture. [As a variation, point to the picture (without naming it) and elicit the word from the students.]

Step 2: Have the students repeat the word. Don't expect perfect pronunciation at the beginning.

Step 3: Give the students practice saying the word while looking at the picture; if they need to, they may look at the word list for help.

Step 4: Have the students practice saying the word while looking at the written word; if they need to, they may look at the picture to remind them of the meaning.

Step 5: Reverse the process. Say the word and have the students point to the item. The students may or may not be asked to repeat the word.

Step 6: Write the word on the chalkboard and have the students point to the item. The students may or may not be asked to pronounce the word. (As a variation, have the students take turns "being the teacher" and writing an item on the chalkboard.)

It is natural for students to learn to recognize a word before they can recall it, and to recall the word before they can use it correctly. Therefore, once the students are familiar with the items on the page and have gained some fluency with the words, it is important that you provide the students with additional information about and practice with the words in meaningful contexts. It is for this reason that the *Teacher's Guide* has been created.

The *Beginner's* and *Intermediate Workbooks* also offer many exercises to increase students' ability with the vocabulary. If you have the *Vocabulary Playing Cards* or *Cassettes*, you can provide the students with additional practice and opportunities for self-study.

THE PURPOSE OF THE TEACHER'S GUIDE

Each page of this guide corresponds to one page of the Dictionary. Words that are boldfaced are in the Dictionary; words that are italicized are new vocabulary that may be useful for your students. To help prepare you to work with your students on each Dictionary page, the Guide gives you information on the following:

- **Notes About the Dictionary Page**

  Sometimes the Dictionary page itself warrants a note of explanation. For example, on The Family page, there is a note that "The family tree illustrated is Mary Smith's, and all of the relatives are on her side of the family."

- **Cross-Reference**

  Certain pages of the Dictionary are natural topic openers and may be used in conjunction with another page. In addition, words may appear on more than one page of the Dictionary. For example, the word **corn** is presented on the Vegetables page as well as on the Plants and Trees page. The Guide may also make reference to a word that is on another page of the Dictionary. In either case, the Guide will give you the cross-reference; the Dictionary page number will be indicated in parentheses, along with an abbreviated title.

- **Supplemental Vocabulary**

  In the event that you wish to go beyond the items presented on the Dictionary page, the Guide offers suggestions on Supplemental Vocabulary. Depending on the page, these words may appear as a separate category or within the Culture or Resource Notes. The additional vocabulary is either illustrated but not labeled on that page or is prompted by the content of the page. For example, for the Houses page, the Guide suggests such words as *carport; skylight; window/flower box; back door;* and *storm window.* None of these words is in the Dictionary and should only be taught at your discretion, depending on the level and abilities of your students and the amount of class time you have.

- **Alternate Words**

  Each illustration in the Dictionary is labeled with one lexical item. However, there is often more than one word in American English to refer to the same object. In addition, variations of words occur in different regions of the United States. The Guide gives you Alternate Words for the items listed on the page. For example, on

the Living Room page, it is noted that a **sofa** is also called a couch.

- **Language Notes**

  Language Notes are provided so that you are aware of features of the vocabulary that will affect your students' learning. For example, a note on the People and Relationships page alerts you to the fact that some items on the page have irregular forms, such as **woman**, which has an irregular plural, *women*. Not only is the form irregular, but the first syllable of the word changes in pronunciation from [wŏŏm′ ən] to [wĭm′ ən].

- **Usage Notes**

  You will want to know about any usage features of an item before you ask the students to use the vocabulary in meaningful contexts. The Guide provides you with Usage Notes, such as the following on the Fruits page: "The word **nut** is used inoffensively to refer to someone who is very enthusiastic about something, such as a 'health nut' or a 'fresh air nut.' "

- **Culture Notes**

  Culture is inextricably tied to language, and an important part of our jobs is to teach the students about our culture. The Culture Notes of the Guide will help you introduce the students to our society. For example, a note on the Vegetables page tells you, "At Halloween, pumpkins are hollowed out and carved to resemble a face. A candle is put inside, and the glowing pumpkin is called a *jack-o'-lantern.*"

- **Resource Notes**

  While the Dictionary presents items with which we are familiar, we could use additional reference information for some of the vocabulary. The page on The Universe, for example, illustrates such words as **galaxy, constellation**, and **lunar eclipse**. The Guide provides you with notes that will help you to explain these items authoritatively to the students. Sometimes this section will be divided into Notes on A, B, etc. if these divisions are on the Dictionary page.

- **Suggested Activities**

    At the end of each unit of the Guide, there are
    several Suggested Activities to help you achieve
    your goal of having the students use the
    vocabulary in meaningful contexts. The
    activities were designed to be flexible, so that
    they can be used in a variety of classroom
    situations: one-to-one, with pairs or small
    groups, or with the class as a whole. Feel free to
    do one or all of the activities, and to adapt them
    to your learners' needs.

Although *The New Oxford Picture Dictionary* is
designed for use with beginning or intermediate
students, it may be used with high-intermediate or
advanced students, especially to fill in gaps in their
knowledge of English.

THE NEW OXFORD PICTURE DICTIONARY

Teacher's Guide

2 People and Relationships

Notes About the Dictionary Page

The photos on this page are from one family's picture album. The first two pictures show two individuals (the woman and the man). The third picture shows them as a husband and wife; the fourth picture shows them as parents; and the last picture shows them as grandparents. The baby in the fourth picture is the girl in the fifth picture and the mother in the last picture. Page 3 has related items (grandmother, grandfather, mother, father, daughter, son).

Cross-Reference

Family (3)

Supplemental Vocabulary

• picture; photograph; photo; snapshot

• There are a variety of terms referring to people that depend on their ages. The ages indicated below are rough guidelines:

Age 0–4	baby: newborn, infant, toddler, preschooler;
Age 4–7	child: little girl, little boy;
Age 7–12	child: girl, boy;
Age 13–19	adolescent: teenager, teen, young woman, young lady, young man, young adult;
Age 19–64	adult: man, woman;
Age 65–	adult: mature adult, senior citizen, senior, old man, old woman.

• The word *kid* is used informally to refer to a child or young person. It is also used by adults to refer to their peers informally.

• The word *friend* is used when a relationship between peers is nonsexual, or sometimes when there is a dating relationship between adults. *Boyfriend* and *girlfriend* are used when young adults have a dating relationship. The word girlfriend, however, can also be used by a female to refer to her female friend. *Couple* is used to refer to a male and female who are dating; married couple (or couple) is another way to say **husband** and **wife**. Before marriage, when the couple is engaged, the male is called the *fiancé*, and the woman is called the *fiancée* (both pronounced [fē ŏn sā']. At the time of marriage, the couple is called the *bride and groom*. For up to one year after marriage, they are considered *newlyweds*.

• The words *male* and *female* are used on official documents (birth certificates, job applications, medical forms, etc.).

Language Notes

Many of the words on this page have irregular plurals.

man/men

woman/women (note the change in the pronunciation of the first syllable: [wŏŏm' ən/wĭm' ən])

wife/wives (this is one example of the f changing to v before adding s)

baby/babies (this is one example of the y changing to i before adding es)

child/children (note the change in the pronunciation of the first syllable: [chīld/chĭl' drən])

Usage Notes	
woman	refers to an adult female; *lady* can be more formal, as in "ladies and gentlemen" or "the lady of the house," or can refer to any female, as in "the lady on the bus" or "the cleaning lady." It is often considered rude to call out "Lady" to an unknown woman; "Miss" is preferred in this instance. A public rest room for females is usually called the "ladies' room." Some people use the word **girls** to refer to adult females. Some women find this offensive, since girl refers to a child, but some women call their friends "the girls" (see below). The word gal may be used informally to refer to a woman or girl.
man	refers to an adult male; *gentleman* is more formal, as in "a perfect gentleman." A public rest room for males is usually called the "men's room." People use "Man!" as an expression of surprise, enthusiasm, etc. Man is sometimes used to refer to all of humanity, as in "No man is an island." **Boy** is used to refer to a man as an informal term, as in "He went out with the boys." Boy can also be used in an offensive way since boy refers to a child. The word *guy* is used informally to refer to a man or boy; sometimes guys is used informally among young people to refer to a group of women or girls, or a group of men and women.
children	used to indicate an age group ("The children are playing in the park") as well as to indicate a relationship ("I have two children. One is a lawyer and the other is a doctor"). When they are young children, we use the words girl or daughter (3) and boy or son (3) to refer to our offspring, as in the following possible responses to the question, "Do you have any children?" "Yes, I have two girls," or "Yes, I have four children, a boy and three girls," or "Yes, I have three boys." However, when they are adults, we say we have "sons" and "daughters."

Suggested Activities	1. Have the students bring in photographs of their family members. Introduce the words *this, these, that, those, my, your, his, her, our,* and *their*. Then ask the students to tell each other about the people in the photos. For example, "This is my baby," or "These are my parents." Students can also ask each other questions, such as "Are those your children?"
	2. Make a two-column list on the chalkboard with all the words for females in one column and their male counterparts in the other. Erase one of the columns and ask the students to fill in the correct word. After the column is completely filled in, erase the other column and repeat the activity.
	3. Bring in pictures of people (individuals and groups) and have the students label the pictures with as many words as they can. For example, a picture of several men could be labeled correctly men, husbands, grandsons, etc.

3 The Family

Notes About the Dictionary Page	The family tree illustrated is Mary Smith's, and all of the relatives are on her side of the family. The maiden names of all of the married women appear in parentheses, e.g., Mary (Jones) Smith.
Cross-Reference	*People (2)*

Supplemental Vocabulary	• The following supplemental vocabulary may be helpful to students:

family (genealogical) tree   middle name/middle initial
nuclear family   last/family/second name/surname
extended family   maiden name
maternal/paternal side of the family   married name
first name/given name

• You may want to introduce terms of further generations, such as great (grandmother), and grandniece; or other relationships, such as stepmother, half-sister, and other in-laws. We have informal ways to talk about **mother, father, grandmother,** and **grandfather**, depending on the speaker's age:

Formal	*Adult Informal*	*Child Informal*
mother	mom	mommy, mama, ma
father	dad	daddy, papa, pa
grandmother	grandma, grandmama	
grandfather	granddad, grandpa	

Language Notes

• We have some words that express either gender, and other words that are gender specific, as follows:

Neuter Gender	*Female*	*Male*
grandparent	grandmother	grandfather
parent	mother	father
child	daughter	son
grandchild	granddaughter (2)	grandson (2)
sibling	sister	brother
	aunt	uncle
	niece	nephew
	sister-in-law	brother-in-law
cousin		
spouse	wife (2)	husband (2)

We use the plural of the neuter gender form as a generic term as well as to refer to females and males. "Many *grandchildren* live far from their grandparents (2)," and "My grandchildren are coming to visit today."

• The possessive of proper nouns that end with "s" can be spelled as either an apostrophe "s" (Jones's) or with just the apostrophe (Jones'). You may wish to explain this distinction to your students.

Usage Notes

• We use the word **family** to refer to both our nuclear and extended families.

• We say "I live with my family," and may mean "my husband and two children," or "my parents (2) and my siblings."

• The term **sister-in-law** refers to the wife of one's brother (numbered) or the sister of one's spouse. The term **brother-in-law** refers to the husband of one's sister (numbered) or the brother of one's spouse. We say "in-laws" to refer to *mother-* and *father-in law*. For relatives other than parents and siblings who are related to us by marriage, we say either "my aunt by marriage" or "my husband's/wife's aunt."

- **Cousin** is a broad term that we often qualify with ordinal numbers to indicate different generations: first cousin, second cousin, third cousin. The correct term for the relationship between different generations is cousin once (twice, etc.) removed. People often use "first cousin" incorrectly for this relationship.

- Traditionally, women take their husband's family name when they get married. Some women continue to use their own family name as a middle name (Mary Jones Smith), or they may create a new compound name by adding a hyphen (Mary Jones-Smith). Some men add the woman's maiden name as well (Bob Jones Smith or Bob Jones-Smith). Some women prefer not to add their husband's family name when they get married (Mary Jones' husband is Bob Smith.) Children's last names reflect their parents' choices (Sally Ann Smith, Sally Ann Jones-Smith, or Sally Ann Jones Smith). Many people follow religious and cultural traditions when giving children first and middle names.

Suggested Activities

1. Introduce the possessive form: Mary Smith's, Mary's, Tom Jones', etc. Have the students pick out a person in Mary Smith's family to "introduce" and tell something about their relationship to another person in the family. For example, "This is Peter Bates. He's Ellen Bates' husband."

2. Have one student ask the question, "Who is _____?" The other students must give as many responses as possible in terms of the relationships illustrated. For example, "Who is Jane Carter?" "She's Elizabeth and Tom Jones' daughter." "She's Tom Carter's wife." "She's Peg Carter's mother," etc.

3. Have the students draw their own family trees (restricted to one side of their family and three or four generations). Introduce the words *this, these, that, those, my, your, his, her, our,* and *their*. Have the students tell each other about their relatives. For example, "This is (name of the person). He's my grandfather."

4 & 5 The Human Body

Notes About the Dictionary Page

Pages 4 and 5 illustrate different parts of the human body. Please note that the reproductive organs are not illustrated or labeled. You may want to include this vocabulary (see chart below) if it is appropriate to the ages and cultural backgrounds of your students.

Cross-Reference

Clothing (19–24) , Medical (39–41)

Supplemental Vocabulary

- Words for **hair** color: blonde, brunette, red, gray, white, black, brown, sandy, salt and pepper

- Words for **eye** color: brown, blue, green, hazel (note that "black eye" means "bruised eye"[40])

- Words for height: very tall, tall, medium height (average height), short, very short

- Words for weight: very thin (skinny), thin (slender), medium weight (average weight), heavy (overweight), very heavy (obese, fat [but the latter is not considered polite])

Usage Notes	There are many common descriptive phrases in the United States that mention parts of the body:

Phrase	*Meaning*
big mouth	someone who talks too much
give (someone) the cold shoulder	to ignore or rebuff
put (one's) foot in (one's) mouth	to make an embarrassing remark
tongue-tied	too embarrassed or shy to speak
tongue in cheek	jokingly

Culture Notes

You may want to discuss *body language* with the students while they are working on this vocabulary, since body language is language-specific and not universal. For example, an English speaker points to his chest when he wants to indicate "me" for emphasis, while a Japanese speaker points to his nose. An English speaker indicates confusion with a furrowed brow, while a Spanish speaker creases his nose. Common gestures include the following:

Gesture	*Meaning*
nodding head	agreement, affirmation
shaking head	disagreement, negation
furrowed brow	confusion, puzzlement
eyebrows raised	disapproval, surprise
finger wagging	scolding
index finger to one's own chest	emphatic "me"
pointing with index finger	that one
shoulders shrugged	ignorance, lack of concern
arms akimbo	impatience
thumbs up	terrific!
thumbs down	terrible!

Resource Notes

The following is a description of the internal organs and a chart of the different body systems.

Internal Organ	*Distinguishing Features*
brain	controls and coordinates the mental and physical activities of the body
spinal cord	the cord of nerve tissue contained within the spinal column
throat	the passage from the mouth to the **stomach** or to the **lungs**
windpipe (trachea)	the structure through which the air we breathe travels to the lungs
esophagus	the structure through which food passes from the mouth into the stomach
muscle	a tissue that contracts to produce movement in the body
lung	where deoxygenated blood picks up oxygen and releases carbon dioxide

heart	acts as a pump for the blood; it is made up of four chambers, two auricles and two ventricles
liver	manufactures bile, which is used in the duodenum (first loop of the small intestine) to break down food; stores glucose (sugar) for later use; where toxins are removed from the blood
stomach	receives food after it passes through the esophagus; it mixes the food while the food is being broken down chemically
intestines	made up of the small intestines and the large intestines; the small intestines are responsible for completing the digestion of food; what is left of the food after digestion passes through the large intestine and the rectum and is eliminated through the anus
vein	a blood vessel that carries blood back to the heart after the blood has given up its oxygen
artery	a blood vessel that carries oxygenated blood from the heart throughout the body
kidney	the organ in which toxins and waste materials are removed from the blood and urine is formed
pancreas	a gland that secretes a digestive fluid into the intestine and also secretes the hormone insulin
bladder (urinary bladder)	the sac in which the urine collects until it is discharged from the body

System	*Organs*
skeletal	bones, joints
muscular	muscles, tendons, ligaments
gastrointestinal	mouth, teeth, tongue, esophagus, salivary glands, stomach, small intestines, gall bladder, large intestines, rectum, anus, appendix
nervous	brain, spinal cord, nerves
excretory	kidneys, ureters, bladder, urethra
respiratory	nose, pharynx, larynx, trachea, bronchi, lungs
reproductive	male: testes, scrotum, penis, prostate gland female: ovaries, uterus, fallopian tubes, vagina, breast
circulatory	heart, blood, arteries, veins, capillaries, spleen, lymph nodes, lymph vessels
endocrine	thyroid and parathyroid glands, pineal gland, adrenal glands, testes, ovaries, thymus, pancreas and pituitary glands
integumentary	skin, hair, nails, sweat and oil glands

Suggested Activities	1. Have the students describe themselves using the vocabulary listed and any supplementary vocabulary you have given them. For example, "I am a tall, thin male with black hair and brown eyes." Students can also describe someone they know or one of their favorite entertainers.
	2. Play the game "Simon Says" with the students. (Simon says, "Put your hands on your waist," Simon says, "Put your index finger on your nose," Simon says, "Touch your toes," etc.)

6 & 7 Vegetables

Cross-Reference *Food (6–18), Kitchen Verbs (31), Grains (60)*

Supplemental Vocabulary

- Not all of the partitives are in the Dictionary. Some of the more common ones are listed below:

head	cauliflower, broccoli, cabbage, lettuce, escarole, celery
bunch	watercress, spinach, herbs, radishes, carrots, beets
spear	asparagus

In addition, for smaller parts:

floret	cauliflower, broccoli
leaf	cabbage, lettuce, escarole, spinach
stalk	celery

- Many of the **vegetables** come in different varieties, as follows:

cabbage	green, red, Savoy, Chinese (bok choy)
lettuce	iceberg, Romaine, red leaf, green leaf, Boston, Bibb
fresh beans	green, snap, wax , string, green lima
tomatoes	beefsteak, plum, cherry
cucumbers	seedless, kirbies
peppers	green, red, chili, jalapeno
potatoes	white, new, baking, russet, red, Idaho
squash	zucchini, yellow, summer, acorn, butternut, Hubbard
radishes	red, black, Japanese (daikon), horseradish
onions	green (scallions), white, yellow, red, Bermuda, Spanish, leek
turnips	white, yellow (rutabagas)

Alternate Words

potatoes	taters/spuds (colloq.)
green onion	scallions/spring onions
cucumber	cuke (colloq.)

Usage Notes

There are many common descriptive phrases in the United States that mention vegetables:

Phrase	*Meaning*
corny	old-fashioned; silly; overused
two peas in a pod	very similar; very close
hot potato	something too dangerous to handle
red as a beet	blushing

Culture Notes

- Fresh vegetables can be bought in a number of places: local fruit and vegetable markets (45), farmstands, farmer's markets, and supermarkets (14). Some vegetables are *seasonal* and cannot be found year-round.

- **Pumpkins** and **squash** are symbolic of the fall season. At Halloween, pumpkins are hollowed out and carved to resemble a face. A candle is put inside, and the glowing pumpkin is called a *jack-o'-lantern*.

- Two vegetables, **tomato** and **eggplant**, are technically fruits. Since they are used mostly in "vegetable dishes," they are often thought of as vegetables.

Resource Notes

- Some of the vegetables illustrated are used primarily as salad vegetables (18): lettuce, watercress, escarole, celery, tomatoes, cucumbers, and radishes. Other raw vegetables, such as carrots, spinach, cabbage, broccoli, onions, cauliflower, peppers, zucchini, mushrooms, and avocados (9), are often used in salads also. Salads are very popular, especially among health- or diet-conscious people in the United States. Salad bars are common in restaurants, supermarkets, and vegetable markets.

- Tomatoes are also used as tomato sauce, a popular element of Italian cooking.

- The most common methods of cooking fresh green and yellow vegetables are *steaming* and *boiling*, which can be done in a saucepan (30) or skillet (with or without a steamer [30]), in a pressure cooker or in a microwave oven (30).

- Some vegetables, such as broccoli and carrots, are eaten *raw*. Other ways of cooking include: stir-frying; frying; or specific types of dishes, such as mashed (potatoes), creamed (spinach), or stuffed (peppers). Other typical American dishes or types of vegetables are listed below:

potatoes	baked, mashed, french fries, fried potatoes (home fries), scalloped, au gratin, hashed browns, potato pancakes
succotash	corn and lima beans
coleslaw	marinated cabbage and carrots

- Vegetables can also be bought *frozen*, *canned*, pickled, and dried.

Suggested Activities

1. Have students plan the dinner menu for their household, real or imaginary, for a five-day period. Students then write out a shopping list of all the vegetables they will need to buy.

2. Ask students to bring in a recipe for a native vegetable dish they would make for a special occasion. Have them describe the ingredients and method of cooking the dish to the rest of the class.

3. Have the students, as a group, create an imaginary salad bar of at least 24 vegetables. Then the students take imaginary plates and make their own choices of the vegetables they wish to "eat."

8 & 9 Fruits

Cross-Reference

Vegetables (6–7), Supermarket (14–15), Common Foods (18), Kitchen Verbs (31), Grains (60)

Usage Notes

- **Grapes** and **bananas** come in *bunches*. We use the word **fruit** to refer to one item, as in "I usually eat a fruit at lunch," when we mean a piece of fruit, like apples, peaches, pears, oranges, and apricots. We also use the word fruit to refer collectively to the food, as in "I usually eat fruit at lunch," when we mean anything from an apple to a slice of melon to a handful of cherries, etc.

- There is a popular saying, "An **apple** a day keeps the doctor away," which suggests that good nutrition is a way of staying healthy.

- The word **nut** is used inoffensively to refer to someone who is very enthusiastic about something, such as a "health nut" or a "fresh air nut." Nut can also insensitively refer to someone foolish or eccentric. Both "nut" and "bananas" refer to someone who is insane. However, the adjective nutty is used to refer to something outlandish, as in "a nutty idea." We use the expression "a tough nut to crack" to describe a difficult problem to solve.

- If something is called "a **plum**" it is very good, while "a **peach**" is a good person. Someone can also be "wrinkled as a **prune**."

Culture Notes

- Fruits and nuts are usually sold in the same places as vegetables: local fruit and vegetable markets (45), (greengrocer [84]), farmstands, farmer's markets, and supermarket (14).

- **Avocados** are technically fruits, but are served in a number of ways with vegetables: in green salads; as an ingredient in dips and salad dressing; stuffed with tuna, crabmeat, or similar salads; or mixed with tomatoes as *guacamole*.

- Fresh and dried fruits are eaten as *desserts*, *snacks* and breakfast foods. Fresh fruit is often cut up, made into *fruit salad*, and served as an appetizer. Dried fruit is often eaten for its laxative effect. Fruit is also available frozen and canned, either in its own juice or in a sugar syrup.

- Fruits are often made into pies, cakes, breads, and other *pastries*. The most popular pie is *apple pie*; we say, "as American as mom and apple pie." Other favorites include coconut custard pie, lemon meringue pie, blueberry pie, peach pie, strawberry-rhubarb pie, cherry pie, key lime pie, banana cream pie, and pecan pie. Strawberry shortcake (18), apple strudel, prune danish, pineapple upside-down cake, peach cobbler, apple brown betty, orange cake, cranberry muffins, and cherry tarts are examples of other fruit desserts.

- Fruit *juices*—orange, grapefruit, pineapple, apple, grape, cranberry, or a combination—are very popular beverages, especially at breakfast. The juice of pears, peaches, apricots, and some tropical fruits is called *nectar*. *Lemonade* is made from lemon juice and water sweetened with sugar.

- *Ice cream*, *sherbet*, and ices are fruit- and nut-flavored. Fruits, especially **berries**, are made into jams, jellies (18), preserves, and butters and used as spreads on bread or toast. *Peanut butter and jelly sandwiches* are common lunchbox items.

- In some parts of the country, families go apple picking in the fall and berry picking in the summer for fun.

- Some fruits are connected to Thanksgiving and Christmas. *Cranberry sauce* is customarily served with the turkey. **Chestnuts** are roasted during the Christmas season; in the Northeast, they are roasted by outdoor street vendors. *Fruitcakes*, made of raisins, nuts, and citron, are associated with the holiday season.

- Nuts are eaten as snacks and are often served with beer (16) at bars. **Peanuts** and beer are traditionally associated with baseball (93). Nuts may be bought in the shell or shelled. Shelled nuts come canned or are sold by the pound and are either *roasted* or raw.

Resource Notes

- Some fruits are seasonal and cannot be found year-round; however, many fruits are now imported during the off-season. Peaches, plums, cherries, berries (except cranberries), apricots, nectarines and most melons (watermelon, cantaloupe, honeydew, etc.) are summer fruit. Cranberries are available from September through March. **Citrus fruits** (grapefruits, oranges, tangerines, lemons and limes) are available all year. Apples, while available all year, are at their peak in the fall and winter. Different kinds of grapes (green, red, black, etc.) are available in different seasons. *Tropical fruits* (pineapples, mangos, papayas, coconuts, bananas, and avocados) are available all year.

- There are many varieties of some fruits: **apples** (McIntosh, red delicious, golden delicious, Granny Smith, Rome, Cortlandt, winesap); **plums** (black, red, Italian, Valencia); **pears** (Bosc, Bartlett, Anjou, Comice); **oranges** (Valencia, navel, Temple, juice); and **grapes** (red, black, muscat, Concord, green).

Suggested Activities

1. Have students plan the weekend breakfast, lunch, and dinner menus for their households, real or imaginary. Students then write the shopping list of all the fruits, nuts, and related products they will need to buy. Have them save their menus for a related activity (Guide 12).

2. Ask each student to bring in a piece of fruit to contribute to a fruit salad for the class to enjoy together. Discuss their choices in advance so that you can be sure there will be a variety of fruits.

3. Have the students, as a group, create a table of at least 24 fruit and nut desserts. Then the students take imaginary plates and make their own choices of the desserts they wish to "eat."

10 & 11 Meat, Poultry, and Seafood

Notes About the Dictionary Page

Some of the pictures (*1, 6, 13, 23, 24, 25,* and *26*) are silhouettes to highlight the difference between the animal and the food. In a few cases in English, we use one word for the animal and another for the food:

steer or cow (67)	beef
pig or hog (67)	pork
calf (67)	veal
sheep (67)	lamb

Cross-Reference

Common Foods (18), Kitchen Verbs (31), Grains (60), Animals (62, 64, 65, 67)

Supplemental Vocabulary

leftovers	broiled	baked	pan-broiled	braised
barbecued	boneless	smoked	breaded	fried
rotisserie	steamed	poached	grilled	

organ meats: giblet; liver; tripe; heart

Alternate Words

hamburger	burger
ground beef	chopped meat/ground meat

Language and Usage Notes

- **Beef** is a mass noun that does not take a plural form. We say, "We eat beef on occasion." Other words that follow this pattern are ground beef, stewing meat, pork, bacon, lamb, and veal. We use "a piece of/a slice of . . ." to refer to a portion of the whole.

- We use the plural form clams, oysters (62), mussels (62), and scallops (62) to refer to the food in general, as in "We always have clams in that restaurant." The word **shrimp** is both singular and plural: "He loves to prepare shrimp," and "I'd like one more shrimp, please." (The plural "shrimps" is also used.)

- We say, "I bought chicken (64) for dinner," as well as "I bought a chicken for dinner." In the first case, we may mean that we bought chicken parts or two chickens; in the second case, we mean that we bought one whole chicken. Other words which follow this pattern are roast, steak, ham, turkey 64), duck (64), lobster (62), crab (62), and the names of fish [red snapper, bluefish, trout (65)]. These words also can be made plural.

- "A ham" is slang for someone who enjoys overacting and showing off.

Culture Notes

- Some students will be unfamiliar with different items on these pages either because the particular foods are not available in the geographic area from which they come (for example, lamb is not used in Japanese cooking) or because of religious or cultural dietary restrictions (for example, pork is prohibited among Moslems). Some students may be *vegetarians* and completely avoid all meat, fish, and poultry, or some combination thereof. Vegetarianism is practiced by people in the United States for religious, spiritual, or health reasons.

- The staple meal in this country is "meat and potatoes." A "meat and potatoes man" is a working man with basic values and a simple lifestyle. The cheapest kind of meat is poultry (excluding duck) and pork, then beef, and the most expensive is veal and lamb.

- Roman Catholics used to have a prohibition on eating meat on Fridays and ate fish instead. Even though this prohibition no longer applies, there is still a common association between fish and Fridays.

- *Chicken soup* is a favorite soup and is sometimes referred to as a cure for colds and flus.

- Whole **turkeys** are roasted (plain or stuffed), and are usually served at holidays and for large family gatherings. Cranberry sauce, stuffing, and yams usually accompany the turkey. In some households, the carving of the turkey is done ceremoniously.

- **Clams** and **oysters** are served raw at *clam bars*. The clams or oysters are shucked, the meat is loosened from the shell, and they are served with lemon and a cocktail sauce to which Tabasco sauce is added to taste.

- When lobster is ordered in restaurants *lobster bibs* are given to customers, children and adults alike, due to the messiness of eating it.

Resource Notes	• **Meat** is bought fresh, smoked, and frozen, at the butcher shop or supermarket. Some meat, like ham, is canned. **Poultry** may be bought fresh or frozen, from a poultry farm, supermarket or butcher. Canned chicken is available, and is used for chicken salad or other recipes. **Fish** and **shellfish** are available fresh, frozen, smoked, and canned from fish markets, fish stores, and supermarkets. When whole fish is bought fresh, the customer can have the store clean the fish or do it at home.

• **Roasts** can be rib roasts (3) or boneless (8). A roast that is roasted in the oven is called *roast beef*; a roast that is braised on top of the stove is called *pot roast*. Different cuts of meat lend themselves to roasting or braising.

• **Steaks** include club, T-bone, chuck, New York strip, sirloin, Porterhouse, London broil, filet mignon, and rib steaks.

• **Fresh sausage** comes as links and patties. "Brown 'n' serve" sausages come fully cooked and packaged and are usually used as breakfast meat.

• **Bacon** is sold sliced or unsliced (slab bacon). Bacon and Canadian bacon are often served as a breakfast meat. A bacon-lettuce-and-tomato sandwich (called a "BLT") is usually made on white toast with mayonnaise.

• *Frankfurters* are made of beef, pork, or a combination. They may be boiled or barbecued. Franks are served with mustard (18) and sauerkraut (18), with ketchup and relish, with chili or onions, or as franks and beans.

• Fish stew and fish chowder are eaten as soups.

• **Lobsters** are a delicacy and may be steamed, boiled, or broiled, and eaten whole. Sometimes the lobster tails alone (usually frozen) can be purchased. Shrimp and *prawns* can be bought in their shells or shelled. They can be served broiled, sauteed, breaded and fried, boiled, and in casseroles. Shrimp are eaten cold in *shrimp cocktail*, shrimp salad, or as peel-and-eat shrimp.

• **Scallops** come in two varieties—bay scallops and sea scallops.

• There are several different kinds of **crabs**, such as Alaskan king crab, soft-shell crabs, Dungeness crabs, and blue crabs. Crabs, like lobster, are considered a delicacy, and substitutes are available that have the flavor of crab or lobster, but which are made primarily of pollock.

Suggested Activities	1. Refer back to the first activities suggested for Vegetables and Fruits. Students may now write out the shopping list for the meat, poultry, and seafood they will need for their meals.

2. Introduce the words *appetizer* and *entree* (or main course). Have students plan a full-course meal, including an appetizer, soup, salad, main course, and dessert, for an imaginary special occasion, such as Thanksgiving dinner for twelve at the White House.

12 & 13 Containers, Quantities, and Money

Notes About the Dictionary Page

This page includes the names of many containers. Whenever possible at least two items are given for each container. It might be advisable to go over the names of the items, which are not included on the Dictionary page.

Cross-Reference

Food (6–11, 14–18), Grains (60)

Usage Notes

- Although we say "**carton** of milk," it is common to refer to the **container** by the quantity, as in "a quart of milk," or a "half-gallon of milk." The same holds true of other items sold in cartons: a pint of cream, a quart of orange juice, a gallon of ice cream. It is also common to say "a container" of milk, a "container" of juice, etc. Eggs (18) come in a carton, but we usually say, "a dozen eggs" or a "half-dozen eggs."

- A quarter of a pound of margarine or butter (18) is a **stick**. If we buy an unbroken package of butter (or margarine), we would say "a pound of butter (or margarine)," but if we buy a quarter of a pound, we would say "a stick."

- **Dollar bills** are also called *paper money*. We refer to dollar bills by their denominations: one-dollar bills, five-dollar bills, or ten-dollar bills, and singles (ones), fives, and tens. When we need change for a bill, we say, "Can you change a five?" "Can you break a ten?" "Do you have change for a dollar?"

- **Coins** are also called *silver* and *change*. We refer to coins by their individual names as well as by their amounts: a **penny** or one cent, a **nickel** or five cents, a **dime** or ten cents, a **quarter** or twenty-five cents, a half-dollar or fifty cents. Colloquially, a quarter is called "two bits."

Culture Notes

Bottles used to be made of glass only, but plastic bottles are now more prevalent. Some states have "a bottle law," which requires that bottles and cans be *recyclable*. Often bottles and cans can be redeemed for 5¢ or 10¢, depending on the state.

Resource Notes

- Juices are sold in bottles, cartons, and individual **boxes**. Unopened cartons must be refrigerated, unopened bottles may be refrigerated, depending on the juice, and unopened boxes do not need to be refrigerated. Frozen concentrated juice is sold in **cans**. It is defrosted and mixed with water to drink. Soft drinks come in one-, two-, and three-liter bottles, but bottled water and juice are sold in quart, half-gallon, and gallon bottles.

- Some canned foods, especially soups and fish, come in individual servings. We often specify the size of the container by referring to its weight, as in a one-pound can of coffee, a twelve-ounce box of noodles, or a two-liter bottle of soda. We can also refer to the size of the item as *regular size, family size, king size*, etc., according to the manufacturer's labeling.

- Supermarkets provide information on the *unit price* of an item so that the customer can compare the prices of different sizes of the item. The unit price is the cost per unit. For example, a one-gallon (64 oz.) bottle of juice may cost $1.92, or 3¢ per ounce. The same brand and kind of juice may also come in a one-quart bottle that costs $1.12, or 3.5¢ per ounce. Both the price and unit price are given on pricing labels. Often the larger sizes are better buys, but this is not always so.

- Equivalencies for liquid measures:

Unit	Ounces (oz.)	Metric Equiv.	Approx. U.S. Equivalent
1 cup	8	1 liter	1.057 quarts
1 pint (pt.)	16	1 gram (gm.)	0.035 ounces
1 quart (qt.)	32	1 kilogram (kg.)	2.2046 pounds
1 gallon (gal.)	64		

Dry Weights
1 pound (lb.)   16

Suggested Activities

1. Have the students name all the items in the pictures on the two pages; for example, "a carton of milk," and "a carton of cigarettes." Then ask each student to add an item to each container, such as "a carton of ice cream."

2. Have the students do real or practice comparison shopping. You can supply them with the information or ask them to go to the supermarket and bring the information in. If the students do the research, ask them to state in advance what product they are going to look at so you are sure there will be variety in the class. The students should look at two sizes of the same brand of a product and report on which is the "better buy." (Note that the students may not themselves purchase the "better buy" when they really shop if it requires more resources or storage space than they can afford.)

3. Have the students, using play money, pay for and get change back for the item they have researched. You can also add together some items as if they were one person's purchases, and have the students practice paying for and getting change back for increasingly larger amounts.

14 & 15 The Supermarket

Notes About the Dictionary Page

This is an illustration of a medium-sized supermarket. Not visible in the picture is the courtesy counter, where a shopper can ask for help; apply for a check-cashing card, such as the one in the picture; get a raincheck on an out-of-stock sale item; pick up a supermarket circular; bring in film for developing; and buy cigarettes.

Cross-Reference

Food (6–11, 18), Grains (60)

Language Notes

Note the pronunciation of the word **produce** [prō′ do͞os] as opposed to [prə do͞os′].

Usage Notes

We have a variety of ways to say, "I am going to the supermarket," such as "I am going to the market," "I am going to (the name of the chain)," "I am going marketing," and "I am going food shopping."

Culture Notes

Supermarkets are usually *chain stores*, with branches throughout a given geographic area. In addition to supermarkets, there are other kinds of food stores: grocery stores (groceries), convenience stores, delicatessens (delis), and individual food stores: fruit and vegetable markets (45, 84), butchers (84), fish stores, dairy stores, bakeries (44, 84) and cheese shops.

Resource Notes

- Supermarkets larger than the one illustrated would include a bakery, a liquor store, and a pharmacy. In addition, there would be a salad bar in the produce section and separate aisles for stationery and cards, health and beauty aids, books and magazines, automotive supplies, and house plants and supplies.

- Supermarket circulars and *flyers* announce weekly sales and contain *coupons*. Circulars are distributed to households and are available at the *courtesy counter*.

- Customers can pay with cash, food stamps, or a **check** (if they have a check-cashing card from that supermarket). In some supermarkets, credit cards are accepted, but sometimes only for nonfood items.

- Shoppers can use coupons from the manufacturer or from the store to reduce the price of an item. Manufacturer's coupons are in product ads in newspapers on Wednesdays and Sundays. Manufacturer's coupons either have no expiration date or one that is several months beyond the date of issue. Store coupons are in store ads in newspapers and in store circulars, and are generally valid for one week only. If the supermarket is out of an advertised sale item or an item for which they are offering a coupon, they will usually provide a raincheck at the courtesy counter, letting the customer pick up the item at the sale price even after the sale is over.

- Most large supermarkets have **deli counters**, which supply cold cuts and cheeses sliced fresh to order, along with salads and cooked foods. At most deli counters, customers must take a number in order to be waited on. *Cold cuts* are sandwich meats that can be bought in packages, or freshly sliced at delicatessens or deli counters. Cold cuts made of beef include corned beef, pastrami, roast beef, liverwurst, tongue, and salami. Cold cuts from pork include bologna, baked ham, boiled ham, prosciutto, head cheese, and salami. Cold cuts made of poultry include turkey roll, turkey breast, and chicken roll.

- Most supermarkets are well stocked with *convenience foods*. These range from "TV dinners" to heat-and-serve canned foods to packaged foods to which you "just add water" and heat. Convenience foods take little time or effort to prepare and require little cleaning up. They fit into the lifestyles of people too busy to cook "from scratch."

- The **scale** in the produce aisle is provided for the customer's information. However, the produce that is sold by weight must be weighed for pricing. This is done in the produce section in some supermarkets or at the **cash register** in other supermarkets. Rolls of plastic bags are scattered throughout the produce section for the customers' use.

- **Shopping carts** are often kept outside the supermarket. Most shopping carts have child's seats. **Shopping baskets** are used by customers who only buy a few items.

- **Checkout counters** and cash registers vary from store to store and area to area. Typically, such items as candy, batteries, magazines and weekly newspapers are found here. Many have electronic scales for weighing produce and optical scanners to read the item price off the *UPC (Universal Product Code) bar code*.

- *Express lanes* such as the one in the illustration are a time-saving convenience for customers who only have a few items. Sometimes there are two kinds of express lanes; for example, there may be an express lane for eight items or fewer and another for 15 items or fewer. This depends on the size of the supermarket.

- Brown paper bags and plastic *shopping bags* are used for carrying out groceries. Small plastic bags are used for frozen foods, and they are placed within the other bag. Some stores have a clerk who bags groceries in addition to the cashier. Some supermarkets have delivery services for customers' groceries.

Suggested Activities

1. Have students list as many items as they can under the following headings: deli, frozen foods, dairy products, produce, baked goods, canned goods, beverages, household items, and snacks. You may want to make a competition of this, breaking the class up into teams to see which team comes up with the longest list of correct items.

2. Have students begin swapping manufacturer's coupons. Students bring in coupons for items they don't use. The first time they can ask each other, "Who uses (name of product)?" and give the coupon to that student. After the initial time, designate a place in the room where students can leave coupons for each other.

3. Have students make up and solve verbal math problems such as the following: "Your groceries add up to $57.83. You have five coupons, for 15¢, 50¢, 20¢, 10¢, and 25¢. What will your change be from $60?"

16 Family Restaurant and Cocktail Lounge

Notes About the Dictionary Page

Picture A shows a family restaurant. Family restaurants serve breakfast, lunch, and dinner, and usually have special children's menus. The food is moderately priced, and service is relatively fast. People can sit at the counter where service is faster than at tables. Picture B shows a cocktail lounge. Alcoholic beverages are served at cocktail lounges, along with free snacks. Cocktail lounges are found in hotels and airports or may be within restaurants. People can sit at tables or have their drinks at the bar. Often people wait for their table in a restaurant in the cocktail lounge.

Cross-Reference

Restaurant Verbs (17), Common Foods (18), Dining Room (29), Kitchen Verbs (31), Plants (60)

Alternate Words

check	bill
cocktail	(mixed) drink/highball
waiter (waitress)	server
tap	draft
soft drink	soda/soda pop/pop

Culture Notes

There are many different kinds of restaurants in addition to **family restaurants.** Some feature a *regional cuisine,* such as California, Southern, Tex-Mex, etc. There are *ethnic restaurants,* such as Chinese, Italian, Mexican, and Japanese, and restaurants that specialize in certain kinds of food, such as seafood restaurants, health food or vegetarian restaurants, and barbecues. There are restaurants that are known by special names, such as *pizzerias, chili parlors,* and *steak houses.* Some restaurants have fairly predictable menus and price ranges, such as *cafeterias, coffee shops, diners,* and *delicatessens.* Restaurants also vary in terms of dress requirements and pricing.

Notes on A	• *Reservations* at a restaurant are sometimes either required or suggested. When making reservations, the caller must say how many will be at his/her table (table for number), the name of his/her party, smoking/nonsmoking section, and the time requested. If reservations are not made and the restaurant is popular, the diner has to give the information above to the manager or maitre d'hotel when he arrives there and wait to be called.
	• Many restaurants feature *Sunday brunch,* which is usually served from 11:00 A.M. to 3:00 P.M. and is generally at a fixed price. The brunch is often a *buffet,* which means that the customers can eat as much as they want.
	• In some states, restaurants are required to have separate smoking and nonsmoking areas.
	• *Alcoholic beverages* can only be served in restaurants that own liquor licenses. Restaurants that do not serve liquor sometimes allow patrons to bring their own wine or beer. At restaurants that serve alcohol, the server usually asks for drink orders before taking food orders.
	• Some restaurants provide *takeout* and/or *delivery* services. In some cases, there is no seating at all and the entire business is takeout.
	• It is customary *to tip* the server an amount based on 15–20% of the bill.
Supplemental Vocabulary	eat out/go out to eat take-out food/food to go tip/gratuity
Notes on B	• There are many different kinds of *bars* in addition to cocktail lounges. Neighborhood bars are places where people go to relax and meet with their friends. "Regulars" are people who frequent the same bar, and "barflies" are people who frequent bars. Singles bars are places where people go to meet prospective dates. There are also bars and grills, pubs, cheese and wine bars, wine bars, night clubs, supper clubs, and dance clubs.
	• Due to the number of fatal car accidents involving drinking and driving, many states have very strict *DWI laws* (driving while intoxicated). Many bars now serve nonalcoholic beers and wines for those who are socializing in a bar, but are also driving themselves or others (as the designated driver) to and from the bar.

Supplemental Vocabulary

Alcoholic beverages fall into different categories:

beer	imported or domestic, light beer, ale, dark beer, stout, tap or bottled
wine	white, rose, red, aperitifs, champagne
hard liquor	whiskey (blended, Scotch, Irish, Canadian, rye, bourbon), gin, vodka, rum
cocktails	martini, whiskey sour, screwdriver, Bloody Mary, manhattan, banana daiquiri, pina colada, rum and cola, margarita, etc.
after-dinner drinks	port, Irish coffee, brandy, cognac, liqueurs, fruit cordials, dessert wines

Suggested Activities	1. Have the students tell a story or stories about the people in pictures A and B. They should set the scene and name the characters; for example, "The cocktail lounge in Picture B is in the (name of hotel or airport). Mr. and Mrs. Johnson are . . ." The students should use the vocabulary listed and any additional words you have given them.
	2. Have students brainstorm all the soft drinks and other nonalcoholic beverages they can think of. Then have the students roleplay a customer and a server, with the customer ordering a nonalcoholic beverage.
	3. Model a dialogue between a person making a reservation at a restaurant and the restaurant host/hostess. Have the students take turns roleplaying the caller and the restaurant personnel.

17 Restaurant Verbs

Notes About the Dictionary Page	This is the first of the verb pages of the Dictionary. If a verb is irregular, the forms for the past and past participle are given under the Language Notes heading. The verbs illustrated on this page are presented in the context of a restaurant, but may be used in a variety of contexts in our speech.
Cross-Reference	*Restaurant (16), Common Foods (18), Dining Room (29), Kitchen Verbs (31)*
Language Notes	**eat**/ate/eaten **drink**/drank/drunk
	pay/paid/paid **set**/set/set
	give/gave/given **take**/took/taken
	spread/spread/spread **hold**/held/held
	light/lit/lit

- The following verbs have identical nouns, and the meaning of either must be derived from context: drink, cook, light, burn, order, pay, and spread.

eat	We use the expressions eat out or go out to eat to mean eat in a restaurant. The word *feed* is used when we give food to others, as in "Feed the dog."
drink	Drink is used for all beverages when we state the beverage, as in "She drinks eight glasses of water a day," and "He drinks wine with dinner." However, when the word drink is used but no beverage is mentioned, it is assumed that we mean alcohol, as in "They don't drink as much as they used to," or "They drink whenever they feel lonely." Someone with a "drinking problem" is an alcoholic. We use take and not drink when talking about consuming medicine.
serve	Used in the following two ways: "She served the other people first," and "He served the salad after the main course." We use the related word *self-service* when we get our own food, as in a cafeteria or at a buffet. The service we get in a restaurant will affect how much we leave for a tip.
cook	A general word that applies to all preparations of food. When we use cook with a meal or a food, as in "He cooks dinner on Tuesdays," we can substitute the word *make*: "He makes dinner on Tuesdays." When we refer to baked goods, it is more

common to use the verb bake (31) than cook, as in "The kids baked cookies after school."

order The server will generally ask, "Are you ready to order?" or "Would you like to order?" Another common usage is to order merchandise from a store or a mail-order catalog.

clear We use clear as follows: "The busboy cleared the dishes," "Please wait until we clear your table," and "Let me help you clear." We also use the verb clear to describe the weather, as in "It's clearing now."

pay Restaurants have different practices when it comes to paying. In some, you pay the server; in others, you pay the cashier. Of course, in cafeterias or fast-food restaurants, you pay in advance. We say, "pay the check."

set We always use the whole expression "set the table" to refer to the general act of putting out the dishes, silverware, and glasses. We use the term *place setting* to refer to a grouping of these items.

give The verb give is used to describe the transaction illustrated, though it is not usually used in restaurant dialogue. For example, a patron would say, "I'd like to see a menu," or "Could you please bring me a glass of water?" At the table, if something is out of reach, we say, "Please pass the salt."

take The verb take is used as the base for many two-word verbs. For example, we use the two-word verb "to take out," as in "I'd like coffee to take out." Similarly, we use "to go," as in "Coffee to go, please."

spread Spread is used with an object, as in "It's hard to spread cold butter." Spread is also used figuratively to describe something becoming more prevalent, as in "The disease is spreading."

hold *Utensils* are held differently in different cultures. In the United States, we tend to hold the fork (29) in our dominant hand, except when cutting, when we hold the knife (29) in our dominant hand. In the latter case, we switch the knife and fork back and forth. Hold is also used to mean to save something for later use, as in "She put me on hold," or "The store held the dress for her."

light We say, "light the candle," and "light the match."

burn You can burn yourself or something else, as in "I burned myself while cooking," and "I burned the counter," or "The pot burned the counter."

Suggested Activities

1. Have the students describe each picture, using the vocabulary listed and any additional vocabulary you have given them.

2. Have the students tell a story in the past tense about the restaurant personnel (16) in an imaginary restaurant during a busy lunch hour, using the vocabulary listed and any additional vocabulary you have given them. First have the students name the list of characters and describe the kind of restaurant.

3. Have the students roleplay the patron(s) and the appropriate restaurant personnel in the following situations: arriving and being seated; requesting a menu and ordering; and asking for the check and paying. To make the roleplay as real as possible, bring in menus, blank order pads, and play money.

18 Common Prepared Foods

Cross-Reference	*Food (6–17)*

Alternate Words

pancakes	flapjacks/hotcakes/griddle cakes
hot dog	frankfurter/frank

Culture Notes

- Sandwiches made on Italian or French bread are called a variety of names depending on the region: hoagies/subs/heroes/grinders/poor boys

- *Junk food* is high in calories and low in nutritional value, and includes candy, pastries, cookies, ice cream, and many snacks.

- Many Americans are becoming more concerned about the foods they eat and are interested in information about the products they buy. Manufacturers also give *nutritional information* so the consumer may know the amount of nutrients and calories contained per serving. Included are additives, preservatives, and other chemicals added to food to extend its shelf life or enhance its flavor. As a result, food manufacturers must list all ingredients in a food product (except dairy products) in order of amount included. Thus, the first ingredient listed is in the greatest quantity, and the last listed is in the smallest quantity.

- Certain foods traditionally "go together," such as franks and beans, hamburgers and french fries, spaghetti and meatballs, baked potato and sour cream, bacon and eggs, ham and cheese, and bread and butter.

Resource Notes

- Typically, most people in the United States eat three meals a day, *breakfast*, *lunch*, and *dinner*, plus *snacks*. Breakfast is eaten from 7 A.M. – 10 A.M., lunch from 11 A.M. – 2 P.M., and dinner from 5 P.M. – 8 P.M. It is common to have a midmorning and midafternoon "coffee break," and to have an after-dinner snack. On the weekend, people sometimes have different eating patterns. For example, Sunday *brunch* combines breakfast and lunch. In some households, Sunday dinner is eaten anytime between 1 P.M. and 6 P.M.

- Typical breakfasts: light breakfast: juice, toast, and coffee; average breakfast: juice, eggs, toast, and coffee; big breakfast: juice, cereal, eggs, breakfast meat, home fries, toast, and coffee.

- Typical lunches: light lunch: a salad or a sandwich; average lunch: soup and salad or sandwich; big lunch: soup, salad, hot entree, dessert.

- Typical dinners: light dinner: a salad; average dinner: salad, meat, potato, vegetable; big dinner: appetizer, salad, soup, meat, potato, vegetable, dessert.

Suggested Activities

1. The foods illustrated can be categorized as breakfast menu items, lunch menu items, dinner menu items, desserts, and snacks. Have the students categorize the 36 items listed.

2. Many of the items on the list, such as hamburger, have variations (cheeseburger, baconburger, etc.). Have the students generate as many variations of the following as they can: hot dog, potato chips, pizza, hamburger, spaghetti, fried chicken, and eggs.

3. Have the students create a menu for a typical family restaurant.

19 Outdoor Clothes

Notes About the Dictionary Page

Most of the outdoor clothes shown are worn in cold weather.

Cross-Reference

Clothes (20–22, 24)

Supplemental Vocabulary

- There are certain verbs that are used often with clothes:

| try on | fit | put on | take off |
| button | zip | tie | wear |

- Types of material for jackets:

wool	nylon (windbreaker)
leather	cotton
denim/jean	fur

- waterproof/weatherproof fabrics

Alternate Words

scarf   muffler
overcoat   coat/topcoat

Usage Notes

- We use the words clothes and clothing interchangeably. We use only the singular form of clothing and the plural form of clothes (cloth means fabric). Thus, we say, "His clothes are always stylish," and "His clothing is always stylish." To refer to one item, we say, "piece of clothing."

- With items that come in two's, we use the word *pair*, as in "a pair of boots," "a pair of mittens," and "a pair of skates." We also use the word pair with items that have two legs, as in "a pair of jeans" and "a pair of tights."

Resource Notes

- **Sweaters** are classified by the neckline of the sweater (crewneck, turtleneck, V-neck, cowlneck), by the fiber used (wool, cashmere, cotton, Ragg, silk) or by the style of the sweater (cardigan or pullover).

- **Boots** are classified by their function (hiking boots, rain boots, riding boots), by the material with which they are made (waterproof boots, rubbers, leather boots) or by the style of the boots (cowboy boots, chukka boots).

- Long johns (22) are sometimes worn under clothes for additional warmth.

Suggested Activities

1. Have the students categorize all the items in the list (types of gloves, jackets, coats, sweaters, boots). Students then add as many new words as they can.

2. Have the students describe each of the people pictured as if they were models in a fashion show. For example, "This is John. He's wearing a flannel shirt, jeans, a windbreaker, cap, gloves, boots, and a backpack."

3. Have the students make up a story about each pair of people in the picture.

4. Have each student bring in a picture of a sweater (or other item) from a magazine or newspaper ad and roleplay a salesperson and customer in a department store, using the pictures as props.

20 & 21 Everyday Clothes

Notes About the Dictionary Page	The pictures on this page include clothes typically worn at work or during the day. The people in the picture are most likely on their way to or from work/school.

Cross-Reference | *Clothes (19, 22, 24), Construction (82), Sports (92–97)*

Alternate Words

blazer	jacket/sport(s) coat/sport(s) jacket
slacks	pants/trousers
sneakers	tennis shoes (Calif.)
purse	bag/pocketbook/handbag/clutch
raincoat	trenchcoat
loafer	slip-on shoes
glasses	eyeglasses

Usage Notes

- We use the verb *dress* to mean "put clothes on," as in "She dressed the baby in a pink snowsuit," or we can use the expression *to get dressed*, as in "He got dressed in a hurry."

- *To dress up* is to dress formally; similarly, we can say *to be dressed up*.

- The verb *wear* is used to describe how one is dressed, as in "She's wearing blue jeans and a red jacket." Another way to say this is to use the two-word verb *have on*, as in "I have a blue sweater on."

Resource Notes

- People dress in a variety of ways, depending on what they are doing and where they are going. For business, office jobs, or "white-collar" work, people dress in a certain way. The man leaning against the pole is dressed in *casual clothes*, suitable for most office work. However, many businesses require that men wear **ties** and **suits**, as illustrated by the man holding the raincoat. Suits are also appropriate attire for women in business, as are **dresses** and **blouses** and **skirts**, such as those worn by the older women in the picture. A more formal work situation would require women to wear a **jacket** or a suit.

- The women looking in her wallet is dressed in *athletic clothes* (not to be confused with sports clothes, which are casual clothes that could be worn for work). Athletic clothes also include clothing for specific sports, such as the running clothes worn by the man in the picture. (See sports pages for more sports-specific clothing.)

- Other types of clothes would be for "blue-collar" work, such as the **overalls** and **hard hat** worn by the man in the picture. In addition to overalls, jeans (19) and **T-shirts** are frequently worn, or there are specific types of work clothes for specific jobs.

- The child in the picture is dressed in *school clothes*. Clothing has changed over the years for schoolwear, and children dress fairly casually for school. Play clothes for children may be a bit more casual, such as jeans, overalls and T-shirts. Female children may wear dresses to school, in addition to parties and other social events, though it is certainly less common than in the past. In many parochial (usually Roman Catholic) and private schools, children must wear uniforms to school. These usually consist of skirts/*jumpers* and **blazers** for girls and **slacks**, ties and blazers for boys.

- **Uniforms**, such as the one worn by the man reading the paper, are common for various types of jobs besides a doorman. Other uniforms appearing in the Dictionary are: nurse (39), fire fighter (42), police officer (43), letter carrier (46), pilot (56) and Little Leaguer (92).

- There are many different types of **shoes** illustrated in the picture. Shoes can be categorized by type (athletic, casual, dress, work), by description (flat, high heels, open-toed), or by specific type (sneaker, pump, sandal, loafer, moccasin, etc.).

Suggested Activities

1. Have the students categorize all the items on the list (women's clothes, men's clothes, workout clothes, shoes, etc.). Students then add as many new words as they can.

2. Have students describe their own attire in class that day, using either "I'm wearing …" or "I'm dressed in . . ."

3. Introduce the words for colors (104) and have the students describe the people in the picture. Instead of naming the characters, have the students talk about them by referring to their clothes. For example, "The young man in the blue blazer, white shirt, gray slacks, and brown shoes is talking to the young woman."

22 Underwear and Sleepwear

Cross-Reference

Clothes (19–21, 23–24)

Supplemental Vocabulary

teddies; corsets; crinolines

Alternate Words

athletic supporter	jockstrap
long johns	thermal underwear
bathrobe	robe

Usage Notes

- **Pantyhose**, tights (19), and **stockings** fit into the general category of *hosiery*. Pantyhose is used as a plural word, as in "My pantyhose have a run in them." We use "pair of" in numbering pantyhose and stockings, as in "She bought three pairs of pantyhose and two pairs of stockings." Pantyhose and stockings come in a variety of styles, including sandalfoot, sheer, ultra-sheer, opaque, textured, support, light support, and control top.

- "Pair of" can also be used when talking about **underwear** as a generic term.

Culture and Resource Notes

- **Undershirts** are either with sleeves (T-shirts) or sleeveless (athletic shirts). T-shirts can be crewneck or V-neck.

- Men's and boys' **underpants** are also called undershorts and shorts. They come in three styles: boxer shorts, briefs (or jockey shorts), and bikini briefs. Women's and girls' underpants are called panties, and come in five styles: briefs, hipsters, bikinis, string bikinis, and high cut bikinis. The same words—underpants, briefs, and bikinis—apply to men's and women's underwear.

- **Long johns** are also worn as underclothes to keep you warm.

- Slips are worn under skirts and dresses that are not lined to keep them from clinging or from being too sheer. Both **half slips** and **full slips** come in all lengths, from mini to evening gown length. Petticoats are underskirts that are meant to show out at the hem.

- Men's and boys' **socks** come in a number of styles, such as dress socks, support socks, over-the-calf socks, knee socks, crew socks, and tube socks. Women's and girls' socks come in a number of styles, including anklets, knee socks, crew socks, and tennis socks.

- **Pajamas** are always two pieces: tops and bottoms.

- **Bathrobes** are worn at home over nightclothes or after bathing. Robes may be practical or fancy. *Negligees* are women's robes, usually sheer and flowing, worn over long nightgowns of similar description. A *bed jacket* is worn over pajamas or a nightgown and is worn by someone sitting up in bed. A bed jacket is customarily worn over a hospital gown when a patient is having visitors.

Suggested Activities

1. Have the students list the underwear and sleepwear worn by men, boys, women, and girls.

2. Pajamas and robes are often bought as gifts for relative's birthdays. Have the students roleplay a shopper and a clerk in a department store, with the shopper trying to buy pajamas or a robe for a particular person.

3. Have the students bring in newspaper ads for underwear that is on sale. They then tell each other what the sale is and whether they think the item is a good buy and why.

23 Jewelry and Cosmetics

Supplemental Vocabulary

wear; put on; take off

Notes on A

- *Birthstones* are semiprecious or precious gems associated with the months of the year (104):

January	garnet	July	ruby
February	amethyst	August	peridot
March	aquamarine	September	sapphire
April	diamond	October	opal
May	emerald	November	topaz
June	pearl	December	turquoise

- **Earrings** are generally worn by females. Some men pierce either one ear or both and wear earrings, and women sometimes wear two or more earrings in each ear. There are hoops, studs, and drop earrings.

- Men and women wear **rings** for ornamental purposes. There are also rings that have special significance. *Class* or *school rings* are official rings from the high school or college from which you have graduated. **Engagement rings** are worn by women as a symbol of betrothal. Traditional engagement rings are diamonds. **Wedding rings**/bands, traditionally gold, are worn by women and men; married couples often have matching wedding rings that are exchanged in double-ring ceremonies.

- **Chains** (especially gold chains) and chains with *pendants* (such as religious symbols, zodiac symbols, etc.) are worn by men and women. Other **necklaces** are worn by women: pearls, beads, chokers, etc.

- Men and women wear lapel **pins** to signify membership in clubs or organizations. Women also wear pins on scarves, dresses, blouses, jackets, and coats for decoration; a more ornamental pin may be called a *brooch*.

- Men's **bracelets** are less common than women's. In general, men wear either identification (I.D.) bracelets or plain bangle bracelets. In addition to other kinds of bracelets, women sometimes wear ankle bracelets, which are usually delicate gold chains.

- There is fine jewelry and costume jewelry. *Fine jewelry* is made from platinum, gold, or sterling silver and may have semiprecious or precious gems. Gold comes in different colors (white, yellow, rose) and different degrees of fineness, usually 14 karat (14K), 18K, and 22K, with 22K being the finest.

- *Costume jewelry* does not contain real gems. Costume jewelry may be made with gold or silver, or may be gold- or silver-plated.

Notes on B

- Women may use **makeup (cosmetics)** on their eyes, face, and lips (eyes: eyebrow pencil, eye shadow, eyeliner, mascara; face: moisturizer, foundation makeup, rouge, blush; lips: lipstick, lip gloss, lip liner).

- **Razors** may be single-edged, double-edged, disposable, or electric. Women use razors to shave their legs and underarms and may use soap or a woman's **shaving cream**. Men use razors to shave their facial hair and may use soap or a man's shaving cream. Women use tweezers to tweeze their eyebrows.

- **After-shave lotion** is for men and may be used instead of *cologne*. Women wear toilet water or **perfume**. Both men and women use underarm *deodorants*, but generally specific products are marketed towards one sex or the other.

Suggested Activities

1. Have the students pretend that they have just received a gift certificate from a famous jewelry store and they can buy whatever they would like up to $2,000. Each student should describe in as much detail as possible what she/he would buy.

2. Have each student bring in a picture from a magazine of someone glamorous in a night-time soap opera or movie who is dressed for a formal occasion. Ask the students to describe in detail the jewelry and makeup the person is wearing.

3. The man and woman in the picture are preparing to go out. Have the students describe their personal routines for getting ready to go out, using the vocabulary listed and any additional words you have given.

24 Describing Clothes

Notes About the Dictionary Page	Items 1 through 16 are pairs of opposites: short, long; tight, loose; etc. You may want to introduce the concept of opposites when starting this page. These adjectives are illustrated by items of clothing, but can be used in a variety of contexts in our speech. The swatches shown illustrate common patterns of fabric.
Cross-Reference	*Clothes (19–22), Utility Room (35)*
Supplemental Vocabulary	• There are verbs related to the first four adjectives that students may find useful: short: shorten; long: lengthen; tight: tighten; loose: loosen. • Different *fabrics*, or materials (101), are used in clothing manufacture: natural fibers (cotton, cotton blends, leather, linen, silk, wool) and man-made fibers (polyester, nylon, acrylic, rayon). There are materials that are blends of the two, such as denim, velvet, corduroy, ramie, flannel, and suede. Some clothing is *permanent press*, or wash-and-wear.

Alternate Words				
tight	snug/skimpy		**loose**	roomy/baggy
dirty	filthy		**clean**	spotless
small	little		**big**	large
light	pale			

Language Notes	**Open** is used as both a verb and an adjective.
Usage Notes	• We *try on* clothes to see if they fit. We say, "They fit well," or "They don't fit well." We can also say, "They look good," or "They don't look good." • Children *grow into* clothes that are too big for them, and *outgrow* clothes that used to fit them.
Culture Notes	• In cold weather, we wear *warm*, or *heavy*, clothes. In hot weather, we wear *light*, or *lightweight*, clothes. Dark colors are most common in cold weather; light colors and pastel shades are most common in hot weather. • Clothes can be **new** or **old**. New clothes may be brand new; old clothes may be worn out. Old clothes that have changed owners are second-hand clothes, used clothes, or hand-me-downs. In most families, children wear the hand-me-downs of their older siblings. • Brand-new clothes that are flawed are damaged, irregular, or imperfect. Clothing that is worn out may be ripped, tattered, torn, or frayed. Socks with holes in them can be darned; suits of wool and like fabrics can be rewoven; and jeans or corduroy pants can be patched. • When we have clothes *altered*, we can have a variety of alterations made. For example, the hem (101) can be shortened or lengthened, the seams (101) can be taken in or let out, the waistband can be tightened or loosened, the pants can be tapered, etc.
Suggested Activities	1. Have the students play a game of opposites, referring to the illustrations, where one student uses one adjective and another has to use the opposite adjective. For example, one student says, "short sleeves," and another has to say, "long sleeves."

2. Have the students bring in clothing ads from magazines and describe the clothes in terms of color, fabric, and pattern. For example, "a red silk blouse and a black-and-white herringbone wool suit."

3. Have the students describe the clothes they are wearing in class that day, using the vocabulary listed and any additional words you have given. Then have the students use the vocabulary to describe something other than clothes.

25 Describing the Weather

Notes About the Dictionary Page

This page introduces some of the words used to describe the weather. The brackets on the thermometer are generalizations for what one might consider cold, hot, etc. There are certainly other ways of considering these.

Cross-Reference

Occupations (86)

Supplemental Vocabulary

- Verbs for precipitation:

  rain (lightly/hard)   drizzle   pour
  snow (lightly/hard)   hail   sleet

- Other adjectives:

  hazy   humid   breezy
  fair   overcast   smoggy

- Nouns for other types of weather:

  flurries   smog   earthquake   aftershock
  pollen count   air quality   hurricane   tornado

- Nouns for weather forecasts:

  extended (long-range) forecasts   five-day forecasts
  humidity   barometric pressure
  wind chill factor   chance of precipitation
  wind conditions   temperature-humidity index

Usage Notes

- When speaking about the **weather**, we might ask, "What's the weather like today?" or "How is it out?" A response might be, "It's raining/snowing," or "It's sunny/cloudy," or "We're having a snow/thunder/electrical/hailstorm." "We're having a hurricane/tornado."

- We use the words listed (rainy, cloudy, snowy, sunny, hot, warm, cool, cold, freezing, foggy, windy, dry, wet, icy) to describe "a day," "a season," and "weather," etc., as in "a cloudy day," "the rainy season," and "hot weather."

- We also use hot, warm, cool, cold, and freezing to describe how we're feeling, as in "I'm hot," "I'm cold," and "I'm freezing."

- When speaking of the **temperature**, we say, "It's 72 degrees." If the temperature is below 32°, we say, "It's below freezing." If the temperature is below 0°F, we say, "It's five degrees below zero."

Culture Notes	• The weather is a topic that everyone in the United States feels free to discuss with anyone, strangers or friends. Major weather happenings, such as *tornadoes*, *floods*, *snowstorms*, and *hurricanes*, are news events that are widely covered.
	• *Weather reports* are available on radio, television, and in newspapers. Weather forecasters (86) are usually trained *meteorologists*, although many TV forecasters may not be.
	• Weather reports frequently mention the chance of something occurring in *percentages*. You may want to review this concept with your class. Reports also might mention storm watches, such as a winter storm watch.
Resource Notes	• Although thermometers have both *Fahrenheit* (°F) and *Centigrade*, or *Celsius*, (°C) scales, the United States commonly uses the Fahrenheit scale.
	Boiling point (of water): 212°F or 100°C
	Freezing point (of water): 32°F or 0°C
	The formula for converting Centigrade to Fahrenheit is $°F = 9/5(°C) + 32$.
	The formula for converting Fahrenheit to Centigrade is $°C = 5/9[(°F) - 32]$.
	• The *Richter Scale* is used to measure the tremors of the earth. A figure between 4.5 and 8.5 constitutes an *earthquake*.
Suggested Activities	1. Have the students recall an important day in their lives in the United States (for example, the first day they arrived here) and describe the weather that day.
	2. Have the students compare the weather in their native country with the weather in the United States.
	3. Have the students listen to a variety of taped radio weather forecasts or read a variety of newspaper weather forecasts and say how they would dress each day.

26 Seasonal Verbs

Notes About the Dictionary Page	The verbs illustrated on this page are presented in the context of the seasons, but may be used in a variety of contexts in our speech. You may wish to discuss the concept of winterizing a house/car, if appropriate to your geographical area.
Cross-Reference	*Weather (25), Houses (27), Plants (60–61), Maps (70–73)*
Supplemental Vocabulary	Opposites: fill/empty; push/pull
Language Notes	**dig**/dug/dug

Resource Notes

In temperate climates, where there are four seasons, **spring** is the time for planting, **summer** for growing, **fall** (*autumn*) for harvesting, and **winter** for resting.

Verb	Typical Objects	Tools
paint	the house (27)	ladder (82), paintbrush, paint, roller, pan (37)
clean	the window (27)	rag, window cleaner (35)
dig	a hole	trowel, shovel (27)
plant	bulbs (60)	trowel
water	the plants (60)	garden hose, sprinkler, watering can (27)
mow	the lawn	lawn mower (27)
pick	the flowers (60)	flower shears
trim	the hedges	hedge clippers (27)
fill	the bag (15)	
rake	the leaves (61)	rake (27), leaf blower
chop	wood	hatchet (36)
push	the wheelbarrow (27)	
shovel	snow	shovel, snow blower
sand	the walk	sand (90)
scrape	the ice	ice scraper
carry	the sack	

Suggested Activities

1. Give the students the first two headings of the columns above. Provide them with the verb in the first column and ask them to list as many words as they can to go along with each verb. Provide examples to get them started, if appropriate.

2. Add the third column above. Ask the students to list as many devices as they can to go along with each verb. Provide examples, if appropriate.

3. Have the students tell a story about the family in the pictures, quadrant by quadrant, using the vocabulary listed and any additional words you have given.

27 Houses

Notes About the Dictionary Page

This page introduces terms and ideas associated with the outside area of houses. Part of "the American dream" has always been to have a home with a front and backyard, the latter associated with leisure activities, such as barbecues, and hobbies, such as gardening.

Cross-Reference

Seasonal Verbs (26), Rooms of the House (28–37), Plants (60–61)

Supplemental Vocabulary

carport	skylight	solar panel	window/flower box
front lawn	front door	back door	side door
storm window	swing (87)	lawn	patio furniture
garden tools	ladder (82)	pool	flower garden
vegetable garden	yard		

Usage Notes

• Whether we live in a private house or an *apartment*, we use the word **house** to refer to our home, as in "Meet me at my house," or "There's nothing to eat in their house." We use home as an adverb of location, as in "We weren't home," or "Go home."

• We have a number of sayings related to houses/homes:
"Be it ever so humble, there's no place like home."
"A house is not a home."
"Home sweet home."
"A man's home is his castle."

• *Gardening* is a popular hobby in the United States, and people who garden are said to have a "green thumb."

Culture Notes

• Two styles of houses are shown in the illustration, but there are many different house styles and materials, sometimes depending on the geographic location of the house: A-frame, split level, Cape Cod, Tudor, Victorian, contemporary, etc. Brick, stucco, wood, clapboard, aluminum siding, and stone are common materials for houses.

• *Mobile homes* are houses that are not built into the ground and can be transported. People with mobile homes live in *trailer parks*.

• *Private houses* like those in the illustration and other one-family homes, like *town houses*, are found in *cities*, *suburbs*, and the *country*.

• Many city dwellers and some suburbanites live in apartments. The apartments may be condominiums, garden apartments, one-, two-, three-, or four-family homes, row houses, apartment buildings, and high-rise apartment houses (45). Municipal housing developments are called housing projects, or projects.

• The sizes of houses and apartments are often given in terms of the number of bedrooms (32): a two-bedroom apartment, a three-bedroom house. The amount of land the house occupies is also an indicator of the size of the property: "The house is on a half-acre," or "The house is on an 80' X 100' lot."

- When we buy a house or apartment, we make a *down payment* and take out a *mortgage* for the rest of the amount of the house. If we don't buy, we *rent*; the owner is the *landlord* and we are the *tenant*.

Suggested Activities

1. Have the students tell a story about the couple in Picture C, using the vocabulary listed and any additional words you have given.

2. Have the students form sentences about the tools on the page, using vocabulary from page 26 and any additional vocabulary you have given them.

3. Have the students bring in the real estate ads from the local newspaper. Introduce the abbreviations commonly used in the ads. Have them pretend that a friend or relative is moving into the neighborhood and needs their help finding an apartment. They can decide how much rent their friend or relative can afford, and how many rooms they need. They must tell the class about two apartments they decide to "look at."

28 The Living Room

Notes About the Dictionary Page

The living room shown is in a house. Depending on the size of the house, sometimes there is a separate room that serves as an office and a separate room that serves as a family room or den, in which case the living room is used for more formal entertaining only.

Cross-Reference

Houses (27), Rooms of the House (29–38), Electronics (100)

Alternate Words

staircase	stairs	**television**	TV
sofa	couch	**stereo system**	stereo

Usage Notes

- In some parts of the country, apartments come furnished with **wall-to-wall carpeting**. We say, "The living room has wall-to-wall carpeting," but we call it *the carpet*. Often people buy area rugs (32) instead of carpeting.

- We sometimes are more specific about **lamps** relative to their placement: floor lamp, table lamp, desk lamp (shown, but not numbered), and wall lamp.

- **Tables** are defined by usage or placement: coffee table, side table, end table, and folding/tray table.

Resource Notes

- **Painting** usually refers to original artwork. Reproductions are called prints. Other kinds of art include lithographs, photographs, and posters.

- **Fireplaces** are sometimes found in houses and older city apartments and are considered to be fashionable and practical. The *logs* rest on *andirons*; the *grill* in front of the fireplace is for safety; and the *poker* (not shown) is used for stirring the fire.

- Besides **recliners**, there are club chairs, easy chairs, and rockers.

- **Drapes** are floor length and more formal than curtains (32), which are usually found in kitchens, bathrooms, and bedrooms.

- *Throw pillows* are often found on sofas.

- The **sofa** in the illustration is a modular sofa, which is made up of individual units the owner buys to make the sofa as large or small as wanted.

- A *love seat*, which is a shorter sofa that seats two, is sometimes placed at right angles to the sofa. Sofas that open up into beds are common. Such sofas are called convertible sofas, sofa beds, or sleeping sofas.

Suggested Activities

1. Have the students design a new, fantasy living room and label everything, based on the vocabulary listed and any additional words you have given them.

2. Have one student imagine hiding an object (such as a ball) in the room and have the other students try to find the object by asking questions. For example, the student "hides" the ball under the recliner, and the other students ask questions like, "Is the ball in the fireplace?"

3. Have the students develop a group story about the young man sitting in the living room, using as much of the vocabulary on the page as possible. Each student contributes a sentence to the story, which you record either on tape or in writing for further reinforcement activities. Have the students include what the young man was doing earlier, what he's doing now, and what he'll be doing later.

29 The Dining Room

Notes About the Dictionary Page

The scene illustrated shows a couple preparing for a special dinner in a formal dining room.

Cross-Reference

Rooms of the House (27–28, 30–38)

Alternate Words

china closet	china cabinet/breakfront
buffet	server/sideboard/side table

Usage Notes

Dishes is the generic term used for all plates, bowls, etc. from which we eat. We say, "I bought new dishes," and "He washed the dishes." The word dish is also used as an alternate for **plate**, particularly when the plate is small.

Culture Notes

- Separate dining rooms are usually found in a private house or large apartment. Homes sometimes have eating areas in addition to or instead of formal dining rooms, such as eat-in kitchens, breakfast nooks, counters, and dinettes.

- Often a formal dining room table can be extended with the addition of one or two *leaves*, which are usually stored under the table. The **chairs** of a formal dining room set are generally *side chairs* (without arms) and *armchairs*.

- **China** is made of porcelain. It is fairly delicate and costly and is sometimes used for special occasions; "everyday dishes" are used at other times. These could be made of many different materials, such as *stoneware*, and unbreakable plastics.

- A *place setting* of dishes is typically a dinner plate, a salad/dessert plate, a soup/cereal bowl, and a bread and butter plate.

- **Tablecloths** and **napkins** are called *table linen*. For less formal dining, we use cloth or plastic place mats and paper napkins.

- **Silverware** is used to refer to utensils made of sterling silver, silver-plated metals, or stainless steel. A typical place setting is made up of a **fork**, a **knife**, and a **spoon**. A more formal place setting might include a salad fork, soup spoon, and butter knife. Like china, silverware is sold as service for four, eight, or twelve. Expensive silverware is also sold by the individual place setting.

Suggested Activities

1. Company is coming for a special occasion. Have the students imagine that they cannot set the table themselves. They must leave a detailed list for someone else to set the table, based on the vocabulary listed and any additional words you have given them.

2. Have the students develop a group story about the couple in the dining room, using as much of the vocabulary on the page as possible. Each student contributes a sentence to the story, which you record either on tape or in writing for further reinforcement activities. Have the students include what the couple is doing now, and what they will be doing later.

30 The Kitchen

Notes About the Dictionary Page

The scene depicts a woman preparing something to be baked. The kitchen is average-sized and fairly modern. It is not an eat-in kitchen.

Cross-Reference

Rooms of the House (28–29, 31–38)

Alternate Words

frying pan	skillet
stove	range
cabinet	cupboard

Usage Notes

A **refrigerator** is sometimes referred to as a "Frigidaire," after one of the original refrigerator trademarks, and as a *fridge*, a short form of refrigerator. Predecessors to refrigerators were called ice boxes.

Culture Notes

- The kitchen is central to many American homes. Although the size of the kitchen and the number of major appliances may vary, sinks (34), refrigerators, and stoves (gas or electric) are considered basic appliances.

- In addition to cabinets and drawers, kitchens sometimes have *pantries* (a room or closet for storing canned goods) and/or a *broom closet* for keeping brooms.

- People generally have a variety of kitchen gadgets and *utensils*. Some of these, such as spoons and spatulas, are all-purpose implements. Others are highly specialized, like garlic presses and juicers.

Resource Notes

- Separate **freezers** can be bought, space permitting, and used for keeping large items or quantities of items.

- **Dishwashers** are optional equipment. Some people get portable dishwashers, which fit on counter tops or have wheels to roll along the floor.

- Small appliances include microwave ovens, toasters, toaster ovens, blenders, food processors, and electric can openers.

- "Pots and pans" is the general term we use for all sizes, shapes, materials, and dimensions of cooking vessels. **Pans** are generally shallow, such as frying pans, omelet pans, and crepe pans. **Pots** are usually deep and have **lids**, such as Dutch ovens, soup pots, lobster pots, spaghetti pots, double boilers, and casserole dishes. Pots and pans are made of stainless steel, aluminum, clay, copper, enamel, cast iron, oven-proof glass, etc. Many kinds of pans are used for baking: loaf pans, cake pans, Bundt pans, muffin tins, cookie sheets, pie pans, and quiche pans.

- A **steamer** (or vegetable steamer basket) sits on legs inside a pot and enables the steam to cook its contents without having the water touching the food directly. A **colander** is used to drain food, like pasta, after it has been cooked.

- The **coffeemaker** shown is a drip coffeemaker; many people also have automatic drip coffeemakers. Older model percolators can also be found in many homes.

Suggested Activities

1. Have the students design a new, fantasy kitchen and label everything, based on the vocabulary listed and any additional words you have given them.

2. Have the students plan dinner, including a salad, main course, and dessert. Then have them list the utensils and gadgets they will need in order to prepare the meal.

3. Have the students develop a group story about the woman in the kitchen, using as much of the vocabulary on the page as possible. Each student contributes a sentence to the story, which you record either on tape or in writing for further reinforcement activities. Have the students include what the woman was doing earlier, what she's doing now, and what she'll be doing later.

31 Kitchen Verbs

Notes About the Dictionary Page

The verbs illustrated on this page are presented in the context of the kitchen, but may be used in a variety of contexts in our speech.

Cross-Reference

Food (6–18), Kitchen (30), Grains (60)

Supplemental Vocabulary

Other verbs:

shred	mash	flip	mix
dice	mince	roast	blend
puree	toast	strain	drain

Language Notes

break/broke/broken
beat/beat/beaten
cut/cut/cut

Verb	Typical Objects	Devices
stir	coffee (18), sauce, hot cereal	stirrer, (wooden) spoon
grate	carrots, beets (7), cheese	grater
open	a can, a bottle, a jar (12)	a can or bottle opener (30), a jar opener
pour	milk (14), cold cereal (18), sugar	spout
peel	cucumbers, potatoes (6), apples, oranges (8), bananas (9)	vegetable peeler, knife
carve	turkey (11), roast, leg of lamb (10)	carving set and tray
break	an egg (18), a glass (13), a package seal	
beat	eggs, batter, cream	egg beater, electric mixer, whisk
cut	an onion (7), a steak (10), a melon (9)	knife, cutting board (30)
slice	tomatoes (7), pineapple (8), pie	knife, cutting board
chop	celery (6), green peppers (7), parsley	knife, cutting board
steam	spinach (6), lobsters (11), rice (60)	steamer (30), lobster pot, rice cooker
broil	pork chops (10), chicken (11), cod	broiling pan, broiler (30)
bake	yams (7), bread (14), ham (10)	baking pan, loaf pan, oven (30)
fry	potatoes, bacon (10), chicken	frying pan (30) deep frying basket
boil	water, eggs, pasta	saucepan, pot (30)

Suggested Activities

1. Give the students the first two headings of the columns above. Provide them with the verb in the first column and ask them to list as many words as they can to go along with each verb. Provide examples to get them started, if appropriate.

2. Add the third column above. Ask the students to list as many devices as they can to go along with each verb. Provide examples, if appropriate.

3. Have the students make up a sentence about each illustration. For example, "The man is stirring his coffee with a spoon," or "After the man put milk and sugar in his coffee, he stirred it with a spoon."

32 The Bedroom

Notes About the Dictionary Page	The scene depicts someone entering a good-sized bedroom in a private house or apartment.
Cross-Reference	*Rooms of the House (28–30, 33–38)*

Supplemental Vocabulary

doorway	picture	shelf (47)	electrical outlet (36)
clock radio	window (27)	house plant (60)	go to bed
fall asleep	go to sleep	sleep	dream
say goodnight	kiss goodnight	take a rest	have a dream/nightmare
lie down	take a nap	tuck in	armoir/highboy/wardrobe

Alternate Words

bureau	dresser/chest of drawers
night table	nightstand

Usage Notes

- In homes where there is more than one bedroom, the largest is the *master bedroom.* The other bedrooms are referred to as "the second bedroom," or "the third bedroom."

- In a household of two parents and three children (two boys and a girl), the parents have "a bedroom" while specific people have "rooms," as in Mom and Dad's room, Jane's room, and Sam and Henry's room. In this case, Jane has her own room, but Sam and Henry share a room.

- *Bedroom furniture* usually includes a bureau, chest of drawers, mirror, headboard, and night tables.

Resource Notes

Beds come in different styles, such as loft beds, bunk beds, platform beds, Murphy beds, high-risers, studio couches and sofa beds. **Headboards** and **footboards**, made of wood, lacquer, brass, or other metals, are appropriate with traditional beds.

The traditional components of a bed are a *bed frame,* **boxspring**, and **mattress**, although some people have a mattress alone, and some a bed frame, board, and mattress. Traditional mattresses come in a number of firmnesses. Mattress sizes correspond to bed sizes: *twin, double* (or *full*), *queen*, and *king*. Waterbeds and futons have recently become popular replacements for more traditional mattresses.

To facilitate bedmaking, the bottom **sheet** is fitted, while the top sheet is flat. Sheets and **pillowcases** can be cotton, cotton blends, flannel, and satin. *Mattress pads* fit between the mattress and fitted sheet to keep the mattress from getting dirty.

Pillows are standard or king size, of varying firmnesses, with fillings like down or feather. **Blankets** come in the same sizes as beds, and provide varying degrees of warmth. The **bedspread** is used decoratively to cover the bed.

Suggested Activities

1. Have the students design a new, fantasy bedroom and label everything, based on the vocabulary listed and any additional words you have given them.

2. Have the students develop a group story about the man entering the bedroom, using as much of the vocabulary on the page as possible. Each student contributes a sentence to the story, which you record either on tape or in writing for further reinforcement activities. Have the students include what the man was doing earlier, what he's doing now, and what he'll be doing later.

33 The Baby's Room

Notes About the Dictionary Page

The scene shows a mother feeding a baby in the baby's room. There are various items pictured that are used for older babies, such as the walker.

Cross-Reference

Rooms of the House (28–32, 34–38)

Alternate Words

baby's room   nursery

Usage Notes

"Changing the baby" means "changing the diapers." A **changing table** provides both a surface for changing the baby and storage space for all the items needed to do so.

Culture Notes

- Parents sing *lullabies* to help babies fall asleep.

- *Toys*, such as those illustrated, provide the baby with opportunities to learn coordination and cognitive skills. Adults play *games* with babies, such as peek-a-boo and clap hands, and recite and enact *nursery rhymes*, like "This little piggy" and "The eensy, weensy spider."

Resource Notes

- The **crib** is used from ages 0–3 years. The **bumpers** of the crib protect the baby.

- The baby can be put to sleep in the **cradle** (or bassinet), which can be rocked. A *night light* is usually left on so the baby is not in complete darkness when sleeping, and parents can easily check on the baby.

- **Cloth diapers** are not used much nowadays, but if they are, they require **safety pins** and rubber pants. (Cloth diapers are still used as cloths for protecting the shoulder of the person who burps the baby and for wiping the baby's mouth during feeding, such as the one depicted.) **Disposable diapers** come in different sizes by the weight of the baby and have a variety of features, such as recloseable fasteners and extra protection for nights. As the baby gets older, he/she begins to be *toilet trained*, or potty trained. Usually, the baby is trained between the ages of a year and a half and three.

- Babies may be breast fed, bottle fed, or a combination. If bottle fed, newborns are given *formula*, a premade milk- or soy milk-based mixture. **Bottles** and **nipples** must be *sterilized* between uses. Older babies are given bottles of milk, water, and juice. As the baby gets older and begins to eat solid foods, the baby sits in a high chair (16) or a chair that attaches to the table. In restaurants, the baby may sit on a *booster seat*.

- Besides being carried in someone's arms, babies can be carried in *infant* or *child carriers*, which are strapped to the adult's back, or in *infant seats*, which are plastic seats with adjustable back positions and handles. Baby carriages (for infants) (45) and **strollers** are used for walking the baby and children's seats (50) are used to keep the baby safe in the car.

- **Playpens** are places where the baby can be during waking hours without having to be constantly watched. As the baby begins to learn to walk, the baby can be put in a **walker** so he/she can move around within the house. Crawling infants or toddlers are confined to a certain area with *gates* at doorways.

<table>
<tr><td>**Suggested Activities**</td><td>1. Have the students put all the vocabulary listed and any additional words you have given them into these categories: putting the baby to sleep, changing the baby, feeding the baby, carrying the baby, and playing with the baby.</td></tr>
</table>

Suggested Activities

1. Have the students put all the vocabulary listed and any additional words you have given them into these categories: putting the baby to sleep, changing the baby, feeding the baby, carrying the baby, and playing with the baby.

2. Have the students develop a group story about the woman, baby, and little girl, using as much of the vocabulary on the page as possible. Each student contributes a sentence to the story, which you record either on tape or in writing for further reinforcement activities. Have the students include what the woman and children were doing earlier, what they are doing now, and what they will be doing later.

34 The Bathroom

Cross-Reference

Rooms of the House (28–33, 35–38)

Supplemental Vocabulary

run the bath/shower/water	weigh oneself	wash
take a shower/bath	get on/off the scale	shampoo
turn on the water/faucet	go to the bathroom	dry
squeeze the toothpaste	use the bathroom	dry off
scrub one's nails	flush the toilet	rinse
brush one's teeth	tank	vanity
plunger (35)	bowl	spigot

Alternate Words

bathtub	tub
toilet paper	bathroom tissue
medicine chest	cabinet
hair dryer	blower/blow dryer

Resource Notes

- A *full bathroom* has a toilet, a sink, and a bathtub or stall shower. A half bath has only a toilet and sink.

  The **sink** has **hot** and **cold water faucets** and may or may not have a cabinet underneath. Above the sink are the toothbrush holder on one side and the **soap dish** on the other. Above these is the **medicine chest**, which is usually mirrored and holds toiletries (23), such as deodorant, shaving cream, and razors, and medicine (41), such as pain relievers, cold tablets, cough syrup, and first aid products. Medicine bottles are often *child-proof* and have warning statements, such as "Keep out of reach of children."

  The **bathtub** is used for baths and showers. Baths are used for washing oneself; for therapeutic purposes, such as an epsom salts bath; or for relaxing, such as a *bubble bath*. Daily showers or baths are customary in this country.

- **Soap** is available in liquid form (liquid soap) or solid form (bar soap). **Toothpaste** comes in tubes or pumps (13). Most people brush their teeth upon rising in the morning and before retiring at night. Dentists advise cleaning teeth with *dental floss* and brushing after each meal.

- Hair care products include **shampoos** and *conditioners* for washing hair and a number of products for styling hair. Electric rollers, hair dryers, curling irons, brushes (32), and combs (32) are commonly used for hairstyling.

- **Towels** are made of terry cloth and come in a range of sizes: bath sheets, bath towels, face towels, hand towels, finger towels, and washcloths.

Suggested Activities

1. Have the students describe a daily routine for good personal hygiene, including care of the hair, the face, the teeth, the body, and the nails, using the vocabulary listed and any additional words you have given.

2. Have the students pretend that someone has misplaced a wedding ring somewhere in the bathroom. Have one student "know" where the ring was left, and the others try to "find" the missing ring by asking questions. For example, the ring is in the glass on the toothbrush holder, and the students ask questions like, "Is the ring on the soap dish?"

35 The Utility Room

Notes About the Dictionary Page

The utility room in the picture would be found in a private home, often in the basement or near the garage. The boy is loading laundry into the washing machine.

Cross-Reference

Clothes (20–22), Rooms of the House (28–34, 36–38)

Supplemental Vocabulary

do the laundry/wash	pour	set
sort	add	put in
load	insert	take out
measure		

Alternate Words

laundry	wash
utility room	laundry room
washing machine	washer
dryer	clothes dryer
bucket	pail

Culture Notes

People who do not have separate **utility rooms** may have portable **washing machines** and **dryers**. If there is no utility room, these objects are kept in the kitchen (broom closet, under sink cabinet, etc.). People who live in apartment houses often have *laundry facilities* in the buildings. People who don't have their own machines or building facilities use *Laundromats* or wash-and-fold services.

Resource Notes

- Manufacturers provide *labels* in clothing and linens regarding their care. For example, "Machine wash separately—warm. Tumble dry—low—remove promptly. Do not bleach." If you don't follow the instructions, your clothes may shrink or the colors may run.

- Dirty clothes are usually sorted, based either on the temperature of the wash, the color of the clothes, or the kind of cycle desired. Each separate pile of wash is a *load*.

Different washing machines allow you to set dials for different *cycles* (gentle, permanent press, etc.), for different size loads (mini to extra large), and for different temperatures (cold, warm, or hot water wash).

Laundry detergent comes in powder and liquid form. Some **bleach** is used only for white clothes, other bleach is made for all colors. Bleach also comes in powder and liquid forms. **Fabric softener** in liquid form is added during the washing cycle. Fabric softener sheets can be added to the dryer.

Some people prefer to hang their clothes outdoors on a **clothesline**. Some clothes cannot be put in the dryer and should be drip-dried. Sweaters need to dry flat or they will stretch. Indoor portable drying racks are used for *hand washables* and delicate fabrics.

After the laundry is done, it must be folded and put away. Some items may need *ironing* (pressing) or touching up. Starch can be added to the wash or **spray starch** can be used while ironing to stiffen fabric, as in a "starched collar."

- The **vacuum cleaner** shown is a canister vacuum with attachments. The other style of vacuum is an upright (38).

- Certain items in the picture are essential in case of emergencies or problems at home. It is important to know where the **circuit breaker** box (or in older buildings the *fuse box*) is and where the valves of the main **pipes** are located.

Suggested Activities

1. Develop a scenario of an emergency situation. For example, there may be a hurricane, or all the lights may have gone out in the house, etc. Ask the students to list everything they would need in each case to be prepared for the situation.

2. Have the students develop a group story about the young man, using as much of the vocabulary on the page as possible. Each student contributes a sentence to the story, which you record either on tape or in writing for further reinforcement activities. Have the students include what the young man was doing earlier, what he's doing now, and what he'll be doing later.

36 & 37 A Workshop

Notes About the Dictionary Page

The workshop illustrated is the kind found in someone's private home, either in the garage, attic, or basement. Most people have certain tools for basic household repairs. The items listed here are basic tools for those whose hobby is woodworking/cabinetry/carpentry.

Supplemental Vocabulary

plug in the appliance	fix the leak
cut the lumber	drill the hole
hammer the nail	tighten the screw
chop (the) wood	chisel
sand the wood	putty knife
paint the wall	hand drill

Resource Notes

In general, there are two kinds of tools, hand tools and power tools.

Tool	Distinguishing Features
carpenter's rule	a ruler that folds back on itself and extends to various lengths
C-clamp	a kind of clamp (shaped like a "C") that fastens one object to another
jigsaw	a power saw used to cut difficult lines or curves
wood	also called *lumber*; available in varying thicknesses and lengths; of different natural origins, such as oak or maple, or may be processed, such as *plywood* or pressboard
extension cord	comes in different lengths; can be regular or heavy-duty
outlet	also called *electrical outlet*; may be two-pronged or three-pronged
grounding plug	may be a three-pronged plug or a two-pronged plug with a grounding wire
saw	also called a *handsaw*; used for cutting wood
brace	a device for holding and turning a bit or tools for boring or drilling
wrench	a tool for gripping and turning or twisting the head of a bolt, a nut, a pipe, etc.
mallet	a hammerlike tool with a head commonly of wood or hard rubber used for driving another tool
monkey wrench	a wrench with an adjustable jaw
pegboard	a board with holes into which pegs and hooks are placed
hatchet	a small, short-handled axe used for chopping
hacksaw	a saw for cutting metal, with a narrow, fine-toothed blade fixed in a frame
pliers	small pincers with long jaws, for holding objects, bending wires, etc.; *needle-nosed pliers* have long tapered pincers and are used to hold objects where space is limited
circular saw	a power saw with a circular blade
workbench	a table for woodworking; the table the man is working on is a portable workbench
Phillips screwdriver	used with Phillips head screws, which have grooves in the shape of a cross
power sander	a power device for sanding
sandpaper	comes in varying grades of fineness and coarseness for smoothing out wood and other surfaces
paint	available as outdoor paint and indoor paint, *flat* and *enamel* paint, water-based, oil-based, and *latex* paint
wood plane	a hand tool for smoothing out or paring wood
electrical tape	black tape used as insulation on bare wire

wire	comes in coils; kinds of wire: electrical wire, chicken wire, bailing wire, barbed wire
vise	a device with two jaws that can be adjusted by a lever or screw; used to hold an object in place while it is being worked on
router	a machine that routs, or hollows out, a surface
bolt	a blunt-ended fastener threaded to accept a nut
nut	a metal block, usually hexagonal in shape, threaded to screw onto a bolt; the "nuts and bolts" are the basics of something (an issue, an idea)
washer	a flat ring of metal, rubber, etc. that fits under the head of a bolt or nut to provide tightness to a joint or to prevent leakage
nail	come in varying lengths and have heads of different diameters; "to hit the nail on the head" means "to be exactly correct"
screw	come in varying lengths; are threaded and have different kinds of heads, such as round heads, flat heads, or Phillips heads
electric drill	a power tool with interchangeable bits for drilling holes of different diameters

Suggested Activities	1. Have the students list the vocabulary presented on the pages and any additional vocabulary you have given in two categories: power tools and hand tools. Note that some of the vocabulary will not fit into these categories, and should not be listed.
	2. Have the students list the vocabulary presented on the pages and any additional vocabulary you have given in five categories: devices used for cutting, measuring, turning, smoothing, and fastening. Note that some of the vocabulary will not fit into these categories, and should not be listed.
	3. Have the students develop a group description about making a piece of simple furniture, using as much of the vocabulary on the page as possible. Each student contributes a sentence to the story, which you record either on tape or in writing for further reinforcement activities.

38 Housework and Repair Verbs

Notes About the Dictionary Page	The verbs illustrated on this page are presented in the context of housework and repair, but may be used in a variety of contexts in our speech.
Cross-Reference	*Rooms of the House (27–37)*
Supplemental Vocabulary	mop the floor; clean the windows; take out the garbage; replace a battery
Language Notes	**hang**/hung/hung **sweep**/swept/swept **make**/made/made

Verb	Typical Objects	Tools
fold	napkins (29), the laundry (35)	
scrub	the floor (32), a pot (30)	bucket (35), scrub brush, scouring pad (30)
polish	silverware (29), the furniture, car (50)	silver polish, rag (35), furniture polish
tighten	a nut, a screw (37)	wrench (36), screwdriver (37)
wipe	the counter (30), a spill	sponge (34), paper towel (35)
hang	a painting (28), clothes (19)	hammer (36), picture hook, clothesline, clothespins (35)
sweep	the floor	broom, dustpan (35)
make	the bed (32), dinner	
dry	the dishes, the clothes (20)	dish towel (30), dryer (35)
repair	the TV (28), the toaster (30)	screwdriver
iron	the shirt (21), the dress (20)	iron, ironing board (35)
oil	the bearing, the hinge	oilcan
change	the sheets (32), the lightbulb (35)	
vacuum	the rug (32), the drapes (28)	vacuum cleaner, attachments (35)
dust	the table (29), the blinds (32)	feather duster (35), dustcloth
wash	the socks (22), the floor	sponge mop (35), mop

Suggested Activities

1. Give the students the first two headings of the columns above. Provide them with the verb in the first column and ask them to list as many words as they can to go along with each verb. Provide examples to get them started, if appropriate.

2. Add the third column above. Ask the students to list as many tools as they can to go along with each verb. Provide examples, if appropriate.

3. Have the students make up a sentence about each illustration. For example, "The young woman is folding napkins."

39 Medical and Dental Care

Notes About the Dictionary Page

The scenes depicted are most likely in a hospital emergency room or clinic and a dentist's office.

Cross-Reference

Human Body (4–5), Ailments (40), Treatments (41)

Alternate Words

attendant   orderly

Resource Notes

- For treatments and remedies of ailments and injuries, people go to the doctor's office, clinics, hospital emergency rooms, medical centers, hospitals, and convalescent homes.

- In case of a medical emergency, people go to the hospital *emergency room*. They may go there under their own power, be taken there by someone they know, or be taken by ambulance (42). If they go by ambulance, they will be examined by paramedics (42), who will administer any *first aid* that may be needed. Depending on the emergency, the **patient** will be taken into the hospital in a **wheelchair** or on a **stretcher**. If the patient is not breathing, the paramedics will do *CPR* (cardiopulmonary resuscitation) to revive the patient.

- When being admitted to a *hospital*, the patient is asked to fill out a *medical history* to help the medical staff provide a correct *diagnosis* and *treatment*. The patient is typically asked about childhood diseases, family history, past surgery, allergies, etc. If necessary, **X-rays** may be ordered, and are taken by an X-ray technician. Lab work may also be ordered. These usually require a doctor's *prescription*.

  If the **doctor** wants more information about the patient's health or suspects a condition, then he/she will order further *tests*: blood tests, urine tests, electrocardiograms (EKGs), etc. *General practitioners* (family doctors, private doctors) sometimes refer their patients to *specialists*, such as internists (internal medicine), cardiologists (heart), or surgeons.

  Depending on the seriousness of the illness/injury, a patient could be seen by the hospital staff on an *outpatient* basis, meaning he doesn't have to stay at the hospital, but sees their doctors and has whatever lab or X-ray work needed done in the hospital.

- A patient will also be asked about *medical insurance*. Medical insurance to cover the cost of hospitalization and other health care expenses is essential in this country unless you are covered by government plans (*Medicaid* and *Medicare*). Employers often provide medical insurance for the employee and the employee's dependents as part of their benefits package.

- A routine *annual check-up* (physical examination) at a doctor's office is recommended. The doctor typically checks the patient's eyes, ears, throat, respiration, blood pressure, *height*, and *weight*. Female patients also have annual gynecological examinations, which include breast examinations, pelvic examinations, and Pap smears (a test for cervical cancer; Pap is short for Papanicolaou, the physician who developed the test).

- A routine check-up at a *dentist's office* is recommended every six months. The patient usually has a cleaning, which may be done by the **oral (dental) hygienist.** The **dentist** uses a dental mirror and explorer to look inside the mouth and probe for *cavities*. If the dentist sees or feels something suspicious, he would have X-rays taken.

If the patient has a cavity, the dentist may administer either a general anesthetic, like gas (nitrous oxide gas), or a local anesthetic, like Novocaine (a trademark for procaine). The dentist has to remove decay from the cavity with the **drill** and clean the area of the tooth before putting in a *filling*.

- In addition to routine examinations, people see the dentist for special needs, such as orthodontics (braces), periodontics (gums) and oral surgery (extractions).

Suggested Activities	1. Have the students tell a story about each of the four pictures on the page, including the following information: Who is the patient? Where does the scene take place? Why is the patient there? Who is attending to the patient? What is happening?
	2. Introduce the vocabulary necessary for the students to roleplay someone calling for an ambulance in an emergency. Make sure the students know the correct number to call in their area ("0" or 911). Each student should come up with his/her own fictitious situation.
	3. In one column, write the name of the area of medicine or dentistry, and in another column, write the word for the specialist. After both columns have been reviewed, erase one column and ask the students to recall the words erased. You can adjust the level of difficulty of the task by controlling the number of words you introduce.

40 Ailments and Injuries

Cross-Reference	*Human Body (4–5), Medical (39), Treatments (41)*
Supplemental Vocabulary	The following are **ailments** (diseases, illnesses, reactions, symptoms) or **injuries** (wounds, aches, pains), along with related vocabulary.
rash	Nouns: poison ivy, allergy, allergic reaction, hives; Verbs: itch, spread; Adjective: contagious
fever	high temperature, fever blisters, low grade fever, thermometer (oral, rectal)
insect bite	bee/wasp sting, mosquito bite
chills	Noun: cold sweats; Verb: shiver
black eye	shiner
headache	throbbing/dull pain, sinus/tension/splitting headache
stomachache	indigestion, cramps, nausea, gas pains, diarrhea, constipation
backache	Nouns: lower back pain, back strain; Verb: back went (goes) out
toothache	root canal, cavity, gum disease, impacted tooth

high blood pressure	hypertension, low blood pressure (hypotension), low-salt diet
cold	Nouns: runny/stuffy nose, watery eyes, congestion, flu; Verbs: cough, sneeze
sore throat	Nouns: inflammation, tonsillitis, swollen glands, **tongue depressor**; Verb: say "Ah"
sprain	Noun: a sprained ankle; Verb: sprain a joint/muscle/tendon/ligament
infection	Nouns: germs, redness, tenderness, pus; Verbs: ooze, disinfect
broken bone	Nouns: fracture, (simple, compound, or multiple), cast (39); Verb: set the bone
cut	Nouns: paper cut, puncture wound, scrape, abrasion, laceration, hemorrhage, bandage (39), tetanus shot; Verb: bleed
bruise	black-and-blue mark, contusion
burn	Nouns: first-/second-/third degree burns, sunburn; Verb: blister

Culture Notes	In the United States, it is very common to have a conversation with friends or acquaintances concerning one's general health. "Hi, how are you?" is a common greeting, usually answered with, "Fine, thank you. And you?" or "Not too good. How about you?"

Language and Usage Notes	A typical dialogue between someone who is sick and another person goes something like this:

A: How are you?

B: I'm sick./I don't feel well.

A: What's the matter?

B: I have a rash/an insect bite/a headache, etc.
   OR
My head/stomach hurts.
   OR
I hurt myself/my hand.
   OR
I feel achy/dizzy/nauseous, etc.

A: I'm sorry to hear that. I hope you'll feel better soon.

Suggested Activities	1. Using the dialogue above as a model, have the students create their own dialogues based on the vocabulary listed and any additional vocabulary you have provided.
	2. For each of the 18 illustrations on the page, have the students tell a story about the person and his/her ailment or injury.

41 Treatments and Remedies

Cross-Reference	*Human Body (4–5), Medical (39), Ailments (40)*
Notes on A	Once a doctor has made a diagnosis, then he/she *prescribes* treatment; *doctor's orders* involve diet, medication, and activity, as in "Take two aspirins and call me in the morning," or "Stay in bed and drink plenty of liquids."

Supplemental Vocabulary

The following are **treatments** and **remedies** along with related vocabulary (nouns, verbs) and information.

bed rest	bed jacket, bed tray, sit up in bed, lie in bed, propped up
surgery	anesthesia (local, general), operating room, operating table, intravenous (I.V.); to have an operation, to have surgery, to operate, to perform surgery
heating pad	hot water bottle, hot compress
ice pack	RICE—Rest, Ice, Compression, Elevation for immediate treatment of an injury (sprain, bruise, swelling)

Notes on B

- There are *prescription drugs* and *over-the-counter* drugs; generic drugs and brand name drugs. *Labels* on medicine bottles specify *dosage*, such as "two tablets, three times a day," and provide *warnings*, such as "In case of accidental overdose, contact a physician immediately." They also have *expiration dates*, after which time the medicine should not be used. We say, "take medicine."

- Other treatments besides those listed include stitches (39), bandages (39), casts (39), traction, and physical therapy. Some people go to *chiropractors* for spinal adjustments, and some people have *acupuncture*, an ancient Chinese technique.

Supplemental Vocabulary

Medicine comes in different forms, as follows:

pills	capsules, tablets, or caplets: chewable or swallowed whole, time release
injection	shot, booster shot, immunization, inoculation, vaccination
ointment	salve, cream
disinfectant	tincture of iodine, Mercurochrome, hydrogen peroxide
eye drops	eyedropper
spray	nasal spray, throat spray
lozenges	throat lozenges, cough drops
liquid	such as cough syrup
gargle	such as salt-water gargle

Suggested Activities

1. Have the students write the list of ailments and injuries from page 40 and come up with an appropriate treatment or remedy. For example, rash—cream. Students may wish to discuss any remedies typical to their native countries.

2. Have the students tell a story about illustrations *1, 2, 3, 4,* and *8,* using the vocabulary listed on pages 39–41 and any additional vocabulary you have given.

3. Have each student bring in the label (or have them copy the label) from a bottle of medicine. Compile a list of all the dosages and warnings and have each student create a new label for a fictitious medicine.

42 Firefighting and Rescue

Notes About the Dictionary Page

The scene depicts a building on fire as firefighters and paramedics perform their duties. Hoses are hooked up to a fire hydrant, which is hooked up to the pumper of the fire engine to increase the pressure. The firefighter in the foreground is hosing down the flames. The firefighter behind him is carrying a fire extinguisher, which contains chemicals to stop the fire. The next firefighter holds an ax, which is used to break through sections of the building that may be on fire. The paramedic is administering CPR (cardiopulmonary resuscitation) to a victim, who most likely succumbed to smoke inhalation.

Cross-Reference

Houses (27), Baby's Room (33)

Alternate Words

fire hydrant   fireplug

Usage Notes

We ask, "Where's the fire?" of someone who is in a tremendous hurry.

Culture Notes

- People take precautions against fires in their homes by installing smoke detectors (33) and keeping **fire extinguishers**, especially in the kitchen. They may also put valuable documents in fireproof safes or boxes. Some furniture is made of *fire-resistant* or *fire-retardant* materials.

- Some buildings have **fire escapes**; large apartment buildings and skyscrapers do not have fire escapes, but are constructed with fire-resistant materials and use metal doors that keep the fire from spreading. They also may have stair pipe systems, sprinkler systems, and communications systems between the lobby and all floors.

- Parking is prohibited within 10 to 15 feet of a **fire hydrant** so that it is always accessible in case of fire. Some streets have a special *fire lane* so that fire trucks can always get through. Fire trucks, ambulances, and police cars are equipped with *sirens* to help them get through traffic.

- *Fire departments*, or their equivalents, are under local jurisdiction; some municipalities have volunteer fire departments.

- The headquarters for **fire fighters** is the *firehouse* or *fire station*, which could be either a hook and ladder company, housing the fire trucks, or an engine company, housing the fire engines. **Fire trucks** (the back truck in the picture) are equipped with ladders, hoses, axes, fire extinguishers, etc. **Fire engines** (the vehicle in the foreground) are equipped with the pumper as well as the other equipment.

- In case of fire, the fire department is notified by a phone call to "0," 911, or the fire department directly. They can also be notified by a *fire box*, which has a pull handle that sets off an *alarm* at the firehouse. If the fire department is called but there is no fire, there has been a *false alarm*.

Suggested Activities

1. Introduce the vocabulary necessary for the students to roleplay someone calling the fire department because there's a fire. Make sure the students know the correct number to call in their area ("0," 911, or the direct number to the fire department). Each student should come up with his/her own fictitious situation.

2. Have the students describe the scene in the illustration, using the vocabulary listed and any additional words you have given.

3. Invite the local fire marshal to talk to the students about fire prevention and safety, including what students should know about how to prevent a fire, how to report a fire, and what to do in case of fire.

43 Crime and Punishment

Notes About the Dictionary Page

The suspect in Picture A is the defendant in Picture B. The arresting officer, in this case a plainclothes detective, is taking the suspect into custody. The officer books the suspect (enters the suspect's name in the police record of arrests). The suspect's fingerprints and a mug shot (profile and front view) are taken. The suspect is put in a holding cell at the police station or issued an appearance ticket.

The second scene is a criminal court. The man has been charged with a crime and is being represented by a lawyer. The judge presides over a courtroom. The court officer maintains order in the court. The court reporter is responsible for recording the entire proceedings. The jury has to decide the guilt or innocence of the accused. A witness is now on the witness stand (see below) being questioned by the prosecuting attorney.

Supplemental Vocabulary

undercover cop; slammer (colloq.)

Alternate Words

police station	precinct/police division/station house
police officer	policeman/policewoman/cop
court officer	bailiff
attorney	lawyer
court reporter	stenographer

The **judge** is referred to as "your honor" or "judge."

Usage Notes

Notes on A

• A uniformed **police officer** carries a badge, a service revolver (gun) in a holster, a nightstick, a radio, handcuffs, and a summons (ticket) book.

• In case of emergency, the *police department* is notified by a phone call to "0" or 911. Police in *police cars* are alerted by a *radio call*. If the emergency is a *crime* (any illegal act), the police rush to the *scene of the crime*.

• At the time of arrest, the officer must warn the *accused* of his/her rights, commonly known as the *Miranda warnings*: "You have the right to remain silent. If you give up the right to remain silent, anything you say can and will be used against you in a court of law. You have the right to an attorney and to have him present when you are being questioned. If you can't afford an attorney, one will be provided you without cost. Do you understand your rights? Having these rights, are you willing to answer questions without having an attorney present?"

Notes on B There are two kinds of *cases, criminal* and *civil*. In the former, the state or federal government is the **plaintiff**. A civil case is generally for monetary compensation.

The accused must enter a *plea* of *guilty* or *not guilty*. In our system of law, there is a *presumption of innocence*; that is, the defendant is presumed innocent until proven guilty beyond a reasonable doubt. The *burden of proof* is on the plaintiff.

The law in this country guarantees a trial by a **jury** of one's peers. People are called for *jury duty*. There are usually twelve jurors and two alternates. In criminal cases, the *verdict* must be unanimous. If the jury cannot decide (a *hung jury*), there is a *mistrial*.

The **attorney** represents his/her client and argues the case. The plaintiff must present evidence and call witnesses; the **defendant** may or may not choose to do the same. When a **witness** takes the **witness stand**, he/she "swears to tell the truth, the whole truth, and nothing but the truth." The opposing side can *cross-examine* the witness.

If the jury finds the defendant guilty, the judge imposes *sentence*, which may include imprisonment, a fine, probation, or community service.

Suggested Activities

1. Introduce the vocabulary necessary for the students to roleplay someone calling the police station because there's an emergency. Make sure the students know the correct number to call in their area ("0" or 911) and the number to use to call the police in a nonemergency situation. Each student should come up with his/her own fictitious situation.

2. Have the students describe the scenes in the illustration, using the vocabulary listed and any additional words you have given.

3. Have the students set up a mock courtroom and roleplay the judge, prosecuting and defending attornies, witnesses, jury, and defendant. You may wish to work out a rough script with the students beforehand.

44 & 45 The City

Notes About the Dictionary Page This is an intersection in a medium-sized city or section of a city called Nautonquit. It is most likely the downtown section, during rush hour.

Cross-Reference *P.O. (46), Library (47), Transportation (54–55), Office (83), Occupations (84, 86)*

Supplemental Vocabulary

- Additional stores: stationery stores; clothing stores; variety stores/5 & 10s/five and dimes; auto parts stores; shoe stores; hardware stores

- Different names of streets: avenue; lane; boulevard; way; drive; road

Alternate Words

traffic light	stoplight
public telephone	pay phone/public phone
drugstore	pharmacy
fruit and vegetable market	greengrocer (84)/fruit and vegetable store

Usage Notes	• When we locate a store, we say, "It's on Main Street, between Adams and Jefferson," or "at the corner of Main and Adams." When something is "at the corner of," to be more specific, we identify the corner with the four directions, as in "the southeast corner of Main and Adams," In the illustration, Lacey's Department Store is *around the corner* from Cover to Cover. The **drugstore** is *on the same block as* the **fruit and vegetable market**. The **post office** is *across the street from* the drugstore. The drugstore is *catty-corner* from the **office building**.
	• The word **street** is used both narrowly to refer to the asphalt area on which the traffic rides (as in "Be careful when you cross the street") and generally to refer to the thoroughfare, the sidewalks, and the buildings, etc. (as in "There are lots of trees on the street where he lives"). Whether the name of the street is "street," "avenue," "place," etc., the word street applies in general.

Resource Notes	• People live in the **city** (urban areas), the *suburbs* (suburban areas), and the *country* (rural areas).
	• There is sometimes a *downtown* section in cities, where **department stores**, office buildings, and *banks* are centrally located, with access by public transportation.
	• The **building numbers** are arranged with odd numbers on one side of the street and even numbers on the other side of the street.
	• The **crosswalk** is the area between the painted lines in the **intersection** that give the **pedestrians** a chance to cross the street. In some cities, *jaywalking* is a serious offense; in other cities, people cross against the light and do not cross at the corners. Safety dictates that people "cross at the green, not in between." Cars are prohibited from blocking the intersections. When traffic backs up through the intersection, there is *gridlock*.
	• The **sidewalk** at the intersection is sloped to allow *wheelchair access* to the street.
	• There are usually **street signs** on two opposing corners so traffic in both directions can read the signs easily.
	• The **bench** at the **bus stop** may be part of a *bus shelter*.
	• The **traffic cop** directs traffic, especially during *rush hours*, in which case the traffic obeys the cop instead of the traffic light. Near schools, *school crossing guards* control traffic to make it safe for children to go to and from school.
	• *Parking* in the city is often a problem. There is no parking at bus stops, at taxi stands (55), in crosswalks, and near fire hydrants (42). Parking is available in *parking lots* (open air) and **parking garages** (multileveled, above ground or underground). Parking can also be found on the street at *parking meters* (meters). A car at an expired meter will be issued a summons (ticket).
	• **Newsstands** are found in larger cities, but are rapidly disappearing. In their place are newspaper machines, which appear along sidewalks of busy streets.
	• In addition to buses, taxis, and private transportation, some cities have subways, sometimes called by different local names (for example, the metro in Washington, D. C., the "T" in Boston). Occasionally, cities have unique public transportation (54–55), such as San Francisco's famous cable cars.

<table>
<tr><td>Suggested
Activities</td><td>

1. Have the students draw a picture of an intersection in the downtown area of a city they know and label the parts of the picture, as in the illustration.

2. Have the students ask each other to locate a store in the area in a variety of ways: by the building number and street, by the street it is on and the two it is between (unless it is on a corner), and by its relationship to other stores (down the block from, around the corner from, on the same block as, etc.).

3. Have the students pick a pair or group of individuals (or one person) in the illustration and make up a story about them, including where they have come from, what they are doing now, and where they are going.

</td></tr>
</table>

46 The U.S. Postal System

Notes About the Dictionary Page

The illustration depicts mail delivery in a suburban area, where the letter carrier drives the mail truck to an area, parks, and carries the mail house-to-house within a certain radius. She then would drive to another spot and repeat the process.

Cross-Reference

City (44–45), Appendix B

Supplemental Vocabulary

mail a letter	open the mail
address an envelope	wrap a package
lick a stamp	sign a receipt
seal the envelope	

Alternate Words

letter carrier   mail carrier/mailman

Usage Notes

• We use the word **mailbox** to refer to private mailboxes and to **U.S. mailboxes.**

• The *U.S. Postal Service* prides itself on its dependability. A quote from Herodotus, "Neither snow, nor rain, nor heat, nor gloom of night stays these couriers from the swift completion of their appointed rounds," is carved on the General Post Office in New York City.

• *Stamp collecting* is a popular hobby in the United States. People can order **stamps** from individual post offices or collection houses, or they can just collect stamps they like from envelopes. Stamps appreciate in value, and certain rare issues are now worth thousands of dollars. The technical term for stamp collecting is philately.

Resource Notes

• In rural areas, the mail carrier drives to the mailboxes, which are on the roadside, and delivers the mail from the truck. In rural and suburban areas, the mail carrier also picks up the outgoing mail from the roadside mailboxes. In cities, the mail carrier either carries the **mailbag** over his/her shoulder or wheels it in a *postal cart* from building to building. In the cities and suburbs, people mail letters by dropping them in U.S. mailboxes. In large office buildings and hotels, there are *mail chutes.*

• The post office (44) is the local headquarters of the postal service. You go there to buy stamps, register mail, have letters or packages weighed to see how much *postage* is required, insure packages, send mail, pick up mail that is being held for you, purchase **money orders**, etc.

- When you are away from home for a while, you can have mail held at the post office. When you move, you can have mail *forwarded* for about one year, but you are expected to notify people who send you mail of your *change of address*.

- There are different *postal rates* for different classes of mail. First class mail is preferential mail, and is the class by which personal letters are sent. Second class mail is slower and less expensive than first class, and is used for magazines. Third class mail is even slower and even less expensive, and is used for brochures and the like.

- Whereas most domestic mail is sent by air, for overseas mail, there is a choice between **airmail** and *surface mail*. Packages mailed at the post office are sent by *parcel post*. **Express mail** is guaranteed overnight delivery (or money back). There are several companies besides the U.S. Postal Service that handle packages and express mail.

- A correctly addressed **envelope** should include all of the elements indicated, including the **return address**.

Suggested Activities

1. Discuss with the students the importance of correctly addressing an envelope, in terms of content—the addressee's name and address (number, street, city/town, state, and zip code) and the return address—and format. Have each student bring in an envelope and address it to a friend or relative who lives in the United States.

2. Have the students tell a story about the letter carrier in Picture A, including what she is doing now and what she will do next.

3. Have the students roleplay a customer at the post office and the postal worker in Picture B. The student-customer may be at the post office to buy stamps, to pick up a package, to get a money order, etc.

4. Arrange for the class to have a tour of your local post office through your postmaster or supervisor of postal operations.

47 The Public Library

Notes About the Dictionary Page

The picture illustrates several areas of a typical public library. The young lady is handing her library card to the library clerk at the checkout desk so that she can take out a book. A man is looking in the subject catalog to find books on a particular subject. Another man is handing a call slip to a librarian requesting either a noncirculating book or one that is not presently available. A woman is seated at the microfilm reader, getting information that has been put on microfilm, such as newspapers, to save storage space. Another woman is reading the bound periodicals in the periodicals section. A young man is making a photocopy of a page from a reference book that may not be removed from the library. The reference librarian is helping a man locate the information he needs.

Supplemental Vocabulary	read	bring (a book) back/return a book
	read out loud/aloud	make a photocopy
	read to someone	fill out (a call slip)
	borrow/check out/take out a book	take (something) off (a shelf)
	look (something) up	put (something) back (on a rack)
	do research	ask for information
		get help

Resource Notes

- The books in the **library** are divided into two classifications: *fiction* and *nonfiction*.

  Fiction books are divided into age groups: children's books, young adults, and adults. Fiction is further divided by genre, such as novels and short stories, and may be mysteries, adventures, romances, historicals, spy, and science fiction.

  Nonfiction books are organized by subject: science, psychology, pop psychology, health, advice/how-to, biography, autobiography, history, and poetry. Both fiction and nonfiction books may be *best-sellers* and may come in *hardcover* and *paperback*.

  The nonfiction books are arranged according to the *Dewey decimal system*. The books are classified into ten classes of knowledge and assigned a range of numbers (0-99, 100-199, 200-299, etc.) The classes are further refined so that, for example, all books numbered in the 120's are on the same subject. The numbers are extended with the use of decimals to accommodate all the books available.

- In order to locate a book in the library, there are three separate **card catalogs**, organized by **subject**, by **author**, and by **title**, which may be combined into a single large catalog. Each card includes the other information on it, so, for example, if you look up the title of a book, it will tell you who the author is. The card will give the **call number** for the book so that you can get it from the shelves.

- Besides books, the library lends records and videotapes. Materials that are not lent out are in the **reference section** and include journals, dictionaries, atlases, encyclopedias, and other reference materials.

Suggested Activities

1. If it is at all possible, arrange for the class to have a tour of the local public library, and encourage the students to apply for a library card for themselves and other members of their families.

2. Have the students tell a story about the people in the illustration, including what they are doing at the library and why, using the vocabulary listed and any additional words you have given them.

48 The Armed Forces

Culture and Resource Notes

- There are five branches of the **U.S. Armed Forces**, four of which are illustrated on this page: **Army, Navy, Air Force, Marine Corps (Marines)**, and the *Coast Guard*. Each branch has jurisdiction over specific kinds of *military operations*. The Army is responsible for land operations; the Navy is responsible for sea operations; the Air Force is responsible for air operations; the Marine Corps is responsible for sea-to-land (amphibious) operations; and the Coast Guard is responsible for coastal operations (in wartime, the Coast Guard comes under the jurisdiction of the Navy). Any of these branches may cooperate in a joint operation. All branches have *reservists* who may be called in for emergencies.

- The President of the United States is the Commander-in-Chief of the Armed Forces. The *Pentagon*, in Arlington, VA, houses the U.S. Department of Defense and the military leadership. *Arlington National Cemetery* is the final resting place for many of those who died in the line of duty and veterans. It is the site of the Tomb of the Unknown Soldier and the grave of President John F. Kennedy.

- In most states, *Memorial Day*, also called Decoration Day, is on May 30 but is observed on the last Monday in May. It is a holiday to observe the memory of dead servicemen of all wars. *Veterans Day* is a national holiday in the United States (and Canada) and commemorates the end of World War I and World War II. It was formerly called Armistice Day, which began at the end of World War I when, on the eleventh day of the eleventh month at the eleventh hour, all hostilities ceased. Both Memorial Day and Veterans Day are celebrated with *military parades*.

- In wartime and during other periods of this country's history, military service has been mandatory for all able-bodied men when they turn age 18. Alternate service is also available in this country for conscientious objectors. This is known as *conscription* or the *draft*. At other times, military service is voluntary and becomes competitive. When you sign up for military duty, you *enlist*.

- Independent of the branch of service, the first experience a new *recruit* has is *basic training*, sometimes called *boot camp*. Military personnel are stationed at *base camps* (or base ports), which may be in the United States or abroad.

Notes on A

The large ships—battle ships, destroyers, aircraft carriers, troop ships (transports), escorts, minesweepers, submarines (subs), and patrol torpedo boats (PT boats)—are naval vessels. All branches of the Armed Forces have fighter planes, bombers, helicopters (57), and short-range missiles. The Marines have amphibious vehicles, tanks and jeeps. The Army has tanks and jeeps. Although the ships are armed, weapons are not standard issue for sailors, as they are for soldiers, marines, and airmen.

Notes on B

Military personnel are organized by *rank*, as in the following examples:

Army	private, general of the Army
Navy	seaman recruit, fleet admiral
Air Force	airman basic, general of the Air Force
Marines	private, general

A complete listing of all military rankings can be found in Appendix D.

Notes on C

The box illustrates small arms used by individuals or small teams.

Weapons	Distinguishing Features
rifle	the distinction between military rifles and **machine guns** has been blurred since rifles have an option for rapid fire; commonly machine guns now refer to heavier-duty weapons
bayonet	a knife that is mounted on a gun to increase the range for slashing or stabbing
bullet	there are many different kinds of bullets, such as armor-piercing (which have sharp, hardened tips); explosive (which have explosive charges within them); and soft-nosed (which shatter once inside their targets)
shell	is the casing that contains the bullet and explosive
mortar	shoots an explosive device; usually serviced by a team of two or three soldiers
hand grenade	an explosive device thrown by hand; has a fuse that is activated by pulling a pin and releasing a handle and that is timed to keep the grenade from going off too close to the person throwing it
ammunition	includes anything that is expendable—bullets, hand grenades, bombs, etc.
artillery	larger weapons, such as cannons, large mortars, and howitzers, that are mounted and serviced by teams
missile	similar to a rocket, carries fuel with it and is usually guided; depends heavily on electronics

Suggested Activities

1. Have the students tell a story about each of the four people in Picture B. They are all new recruits. The students should use the vocabulary listed and any additional words you have given.

2. Have the students ask each other questions about the armed forces, beginning with "Which branch?" such as, "Which branch has sailors?"

49 Trucks

Cross-Reference	*Highway (53)*
Supplemental Vocabulary	truck stop

Kind of Truck	Distinguishing Features
street cleaner	has a broom and sprayer; rides along the curb, sweeping trash as it goes
tow truck	has rigging in the back so that it can pull another vehicle; sometimes it has a hydraulic platform to carry another vehicle
fuel truck	delivers fuel to gas stations or private consumers; its contents are extremely flammable
pickup truck	usually a private vehicle used for transporting light equipment and goods
snow plow	a truck with a plow attached in front that is used to push snow to the side of the road
garbage truck	may be used by a public or private carter; has a chute in the rear into which the **sanitation worker** empties the trash can
lunch truck	parked near a construction site, office building, or amusement area, such as a beach, so that people can easily buy coffee, sandwiches, and snacks during their workday
panel truck	used mainly to deliver light or small objects
moving van	of different sizes, depending on the number of items to be moved; people either contract with professional **movers** or rent moving vans and do it themselves
cement truck (82)	has a cement mixer that combines clay or shale with powdered limestone and water to make cement, and from which cement is poured
dump truck	has a dump body designed for the transportation and dumping of loose materials, such as sand or coal
tractor trailer	the tractor or cab is the motorized part, which is hitched to the trailer where cargo is stored; in an accident, a tractor trailer may jackknife
transporter	truck used to carry cars or boats
flatbed	has a flat platform for carrying cargo, such as logs, or other vehicles

Suggested Activities	1. Have the students ask each other questions about the trucks, beginning with "Which truck?" such as, "Which truck pulls other vehicles?"
	2. Have each student pick out one of the trucks and tell a story about a typical workday for the truck driver.

50 & 51 Cars

Cars are an important part of American life. Unless one lives close to a major city, cars are vital to survival in most areas. Cars come in many varieties of sizes and styles, only a few of which are illustrated in the Dictionary. They may be two-door or four-door, hatchbacks or sedans, and have automatic or manual transmissions. People drive family cars, sports cars (53), station wagons, minivans, vans (53), light trucks, and jeeps (48). Cars are sold with some standard features and many options.

Cross-Reference

Highway (53)

**Supplemental
Vocabulary**

high beams; hazard lights

Alternate Words

car	auto(mobile)
bumper	fender
manual transmission	standard transmission
turn signal lights	directional lights
parking lights	fog lights
taillight	rear light
spare tire	spare

Usage Notes

• "Back seat driver" refers to someone who tells the driver what to do from the back seat of the car.

• When we want the driver to go fast, we say, "Step on it." When we want the driver to stop fast (stop short), we say, "Hit the brakes."

• Minor accidents where the car is slightly damaged are called *fender benders*.

Culture Notes

Driving privileges are under state jurisdiction. In most states, people can legally drive after they turn 16 if they get a *driver's license*. Each state has its own *driving test*, usually in two parts: a written test and a road test. If a person moves from one state to another, he/she must pass that state's driving test to get that state's driver's license. Driver's licenses only last for a certain number of years and must be renewed. Many driver's licenses now come with photos, and they are often used as a form of *identification* (I.D.).

Notes on A and B

• The **dashboard** of the car is equipped with a number of devices to allow the driver to monitor the car while driving. *Warning lights*, written warning messages, and spoken (computer voice) warning messages let the driver know if there is a potentially dangerous condition, such as "out of gas."

• The **gas gauge** indicates how much fuel is in the **gas tank**. The **speedometer** indicates the speed of the car in *miles per hour* and sometimes kilometers per hour. The *temperature gauge* indicates how hot the **engine** is running, from cold to hot, based on the temperature of the coolant in the radiator. The *ammeter* or *voltmeter* indicates how much electric current is being generated by the **battery**. The *tachometer* indicates how fast the engine is going, measured in revolutions per minute (RPMs). The *oil gauge* indicates how much oil is in the engine, from low to high. The *odometer* indicates the distance traveled.

- The temperature and air controls are also on the dashboard. Cars usually have heating systems and a *defroster*. Many cars now have air conditioning. Some cars have rear defrosters for the rear windshields.

- In a car with an **automatic transmission** (an automatic), the **gearshift** allows you to be in park, drive 1, drive 2, neutral, and reverse. In a car with a **manual transmission** (a standard transmission, a stick shift, four-on-the-floor), the **stick shift** allows you to go from first gear to second to third to fourth (in some cars, to fifth), and reverse, with neutral being the home position of the stick. In order to shift gears with a manual transmission you must use a **clutch**.

- The **emergency brake** is controlled by a foot pedal or by a hand lever, in which case it is also called a hand brake.

Notes on C

- The lights are controlled from the dashboard. **Backup lights** go on automatically when the car is in reverse. **Brake lights** go on automatically when the **brakes** are applied.

- The front seat has a *driver's seat* and a *passenger seat*. The **child's seat** is usually attached to the back seat and is a safety feature for infants and toddlers. Children's seats are mandatory in some states. Similarly, **seat belts**—waist or shoulder harness styles—must be worn by the front seat occupants in some states.

Notes on D and E

- The **trunk** of a car is equipped with a jack, a tire iron, and a spare tire for changing a flat tire. After the car is jacked up and secure, the hubcap is removed, the lugnuts are removed, the wheel is removed, the spare is put on, and then the process reversed. Different kinds of **tires**, such as radials, all-weather tires, and snow tires, are available.

- **License plates** are required by law. Each state has distinct license plates in terms of color, numbering system, state motto, and insignia. Special license plates are issued to handicapped persons, police, medical doctors, diplomats, etc. People can opt to get vanity plates, which often spell out the name of the car owner.

- State laws require that cars be registered and insured. Cars must pass *inspections* that verify that lights, windshield wipers, brakes, etc. are in working order, and that the exhaust system meets emission standards. *Registrations* are stamped by the inspector.

Notes on F

Routine *maintenance* includes checking the level of the water in the battery, the coolant in the radiator, the oil in the engine, the air in tires, the transmission fluid, and the brake fluid. The air filter, fan belts, and hoses need to be changed with time. Periodically a *tune-up* and an *oil change* need to be done.

Suggested Activities

1. Have the students bring in a picture of a car from a magazine. In pairs, have them roleplay a car buyer and car dealer, using the picture as a prop.

2. Have the students list all the parts of the car that are safety features, such as door locks, side mirror, windshield wiper, rearview mirror, etc.

3. Write the following headings on the chalkboard: part of the interior, under the hood, in the trunk, part of the body. Write the words on 58 individual index cards and mix them up. Have the students take turns picking a card and writing the word(s) under the correct heading on the board.

52 Bikes

Supplemental Vocabulary

There are a variety of bikes, some of which are illustrated on this page:
two-wheeler; 10-speed; touring bike; racing bike; bicycle-built-for-two; 3-speed

Alternate Words

bike   bicycle
seat   saddle

Culture Notes

- **Bicycle** riding is becoming more and more popular in the United States. Bike racing is better known, and more people are using bicycles as a way to maintain their health or for recreation. Bicycles are also used in large cities by bike messengers, and many people are using bicycles as an alternative means of transportation to and from work or shopping.

- Bike Safety: Certain *safety measures* should be taken by bicyclists. They should: wear a **helmet** to protect against head injuries in case of accident; obey all traffic rules (same rules for cars); ride with the flow of traffic; and use hand signals for turning and stopping. Although bikes have the right of way over cars, it is better to assume that the driver of the car cannot see the bike. Wear *reflective clothing* (jackets, ankle bands) so that drivers can better see you. Remember to use side, front, and rear **reflectors** and headlights for night riding. Some states require helmets and full reflector/headlight kits.

Resource Notes

Parts of a Bicycle	*Distinguishing Features*
seat	styled differently for males, females, and type of bike
frame	styled differently for males, females, and type of bike
fender	found on children's bikes and some 10-speeds
brake	front and rear brakes that stop the tires; controlled by **hand brakes** (brake handles) or foot brakes (pedals)
gears	made up of a front and rear gear; the gears have **sprockets** (teeth) that mesh with the **chain**; gears are shifted to enable the rider to go faster or uphill
gear changer	also called gear change handle; causes the derailleurs (front and rear) to move the chain from gear to gear
cable	connects the hand brakes to the front and rear brakes and connects the gear changer to the derailleur
wheel	made up of a hub, spoke, and rim
tire	fits on the rim of the wheel; the inner tube of the tire actually holds the air; the **valve** is part of the inner tube through which the air is pumped

Suggested Activities

1. Have the students bring in a picture of a bike from a magazine and label all the parts of the bike.

2. Have the students tell a story about the children in the picture at the top of the page, using the vocabulary listed and any additional words you have given.

3. Have the students describe the ideal kind of bicycle or motorcycle they would like to own.

53 Highway Travel

Notes About the Dictionary Page

The scene depicts a cloverleaf on a toll highway. A cloverleaf is a typically American construction where two major roadways intersect. It is also convenient for making U-turns.

Cross-Reference

City (44–45), Trucks (49), Cars (50–51)

Supplemental Vocabulary

- There are many different names for highways, depending on the state or region: freeways; expressways; thruways; turnpikes (usually a toll road); and parkways (usually for noncommercial traffic only).

divided highway	signal	get on	pay a toll
drive (97)	brake	get off	get gas
pass	tailgate	exit	fill up
change lanes	hitchhike	take an exit	check the oil

Alternate Words

service station	gas station
cloverleaf	interchange

Culture Notes

Highway travel is a popular way to go long distances in the United States. Many people travel on the highways for their vacations to "see America." People enjoy going out on the "open road," and highways are often the quickest ways to get to the places they're going.

Resource Notes

- **Interstate highways** are multilane, divided roads that have no traffic lights, have limited access and cross state borders. The same-shaped, red-and-blue road sign is used throughout the United States for interstate highways. These roads are numbered, with even numbers being east/west routes, and odd numbers north/south. They are called I + number, as in I 40, or simply "the interstate."

- Other divided highways are U.S. or *state highways* and are called either U.S. + number or Route + number, as in U.S. 1 or Route 1. These road signs are usually black and white.

- When you enter a *toll road*, you get a ticket at a **tollbooth**, and when you exit, you pay the amount due depending on the distance driven; on other types of toll roads there is a tollbooth every x-number of miles, and you have to pay a certain amount each time. With the latter arrangement, there may be special lanes for exact change or a token. In other lanes, there will be a *toll collector*.

- Roads are characterized by the number of lanes of traffic they allow in one direction, as in a three-lane highway, or a six-lane freeway. On a three-lane highway, the **right lane** is for entering vehicles and slow vehicles; the **left lane** is for passing, and trucks are not allowed in the left lane. Lanes are usually separated by broken white or yellow lines. A solid white or yellow line indicates no passing from that lane to another. (A double yellow line separates the two directions of traffic on undivided highways.) Some roads have special lanes; for example, during rush hour, a lane may be designated as a bus lane only.

- The **center divider** is often constructed of special material and in a particular shape to absorb or deflect the impact of a car that is out of control so that the car cannot cross over to oncoming traffic. If a car becomes disabled, the driver pulls off onto the **shoulder** of the road, which in most cases is to the far right and sometimes referred to as the breakdown lane.

- Certain kinds of vehicles are *prohibited* from certain roads. For example, commercial traffic may be prohibited. In certain weather conditions, certain kinds of restrictions may apply. For example, in high winds, car-pulled trailers and motorcycles may be banned.

- Highway driving differs from other types of driving, since it is faster, and there are fewer opportunities for stopping and turning. Signs are posted on the road to advise and warn motorists. **Road signs** give the route number; junction/ interchange signs advise of an upcoming connecting road; **exit signs** give the driver time to get into the proper lane for exiting, etc.

- *Exits* are sometimes numbered. There is sometimes an extra lane a few hundred feet before the exit and after the entrance to lessen the disruption to traffic of cars getting on and off the highway. On some very busy freeways there is a traffic light at the entrance to control the number and timing of cars getting on the freeway.

- The speed limit is posted on a **speed limit sign**. The national speed limit of 55 mph has been in force since 1975, though some states are changing this limit on certain highways.

- On some highways there are **service areas** on the side of the road for easy on/off access. These appear along the highway at specified intervals. They usually include a *service station* and a restaurant (16) or *snack bar*. At the gas station, you can fill your car up at either a self-service, express service, or full-service pump. The *attendant* will want to know if you are paying by cash or credit card. You can also use the **air pump** (air hose) to fill your tires, and the squeegee or wipes to clean off your windshield (50) and windows. There are also *rest areas* along some highways, which usually just include bathrooms.

- Hitchhiking (or picking up a **hitchhiker**) is illegal in some states/on some roads.

Suggested Activities	1. Bring in a road map of your area. Instruct the students in how to read the legend so they can identify the different kinds of highways on the map. Ask them to list several major highways in their area. In the next column, ask them to indicate whether it is a toll road or not. In the next column, ask them to write the two furthest points the road connects.

2. Have one student roleplay someone who needs directions to a well-known place within a short drive (for example, a shopping mall) and another student roleplay a gas station attendant who gives directions. If appropriate, provide a model for the dialogue, and/or a hand-drawn (fictitious) map.

3. Have one student roleplay someone who needs gas and another student a gas station attendant. If appropriate, provide a model for the dialogue.

54 & 55 Public Transportation

Cross-Reference | *City (44–45)*

Usage Notes | Regardless of the kind of transportation, we use the words **passenger** and **fare**. *Mass transit* refers to **buses**, **subways**, and commuter lines. We use the words catch, board, and miss with buses, subways, and trains.

Notes on A
- The picture illustrates a **passenger** asking the **bus driver** for a **transfer**, which would allow him to switch to another bus. On most buses, the seats nearest the doors are reserved for the handicapped or elderly, indicated by the handicapped symbol.

- Buses may be local buses or *commuter buses*. Commuter buses take riders from the suburbs and outlying areas into the city. The **fare** may be the same for all passengers, or depend on the distance travelled. Passengers must have *exact change* (in coin) on buses where bus drivers do not make change. In some places, monthly bus passes are available and save money for regular bus riders.

Notes on B
- The picture illustrates the inside of a **subway car** and a subway station (44), showing a train pulling up to the **platform**. The **conductor** is the person who makes announcements, collects fares, if applicable, and controls the doors of the cars. The *engineer* drives the subway train.

- Subways travel specific routes, which are called *lines*. The names of each line may be numbers, letters, colors, destination, etc.

- Passengers who stand during the subway ride can hold onto poles, hold onto seat backs, or hang onto straps (a word still in use though they are no longer made of leather). However, the word straphanger refers to all subway passengers.

- The fare may be the same for all passengers or depend on the distance travelled. Although most have **turnstiles**, different subway systems have different systems for paying the fare (tokens, cards, or coins). The token is purchased at a **token booth** or at a machine; the person who sells tokens is called the token booth clerk.

- For reasons of safety, passengers waiting for a train should stand behind the line painted on the platform so there is no danger of their falling onto the **track**.

Usage Notes | The underground train in a city may be called the subway, the metro, or by a local name (e.g., the "T"). When a train rides above the ground on elevated tracks, it is called the "el."

Notes on C
- The scene depicted is of a **commuter train** pulling into a station. Commuter trains take **commuters** from the suburbs and outlying areas to the city. The term train **station** applies to the local stations as well as to the main station in the city from which all the trains originate.

- Commuters can wait for their trains outdoors on the platform or inside the *waiting room*. Commuter trains operate according to a **timetable**, although they are not always on schedule.

- Commuter trains sometimes have special cars: smoking cars, nonsmoking cars, and club cars, where refreshments are sold. The seats in commuter trains are often adjustable so they can be made to face either direction.

- The fare varies depending on the distance travelled. **Tickets** can be purchased in the station at the **ticket window** or on the train from the conductor. (Sometimes a fine is charged if the ticket is bought on the train when there is a ticket seller at the station.) The fare depends also on the time of day; the fare during *peak time* or rush hour is more expensive than during *off-peak*. Passengers may purchase *one-way* or *round-trip* tickets, with the latter being less expensive than two one-way tickets. Commuters often buy *monthly tickets*, which also represent a discount over the fare purchased on a daily basis.

Notes on D

- The pictures depict a close-up of a taxi **meter** and a passenger getting into a **taxi** at a **taxi stand**.

- In some communities, you must phone for a cab; in other communities, you can hail a cab. In some places, there are taxi stands; in others, there are private cab companies with storefronts where you can get a cab.

- Taxi fares depend on the distance traveled and sometimes on the number of passengers in the car. In some communities, the fare is based on the **meter**, which also factors in the amount of time you are using the cab. Where meters are not used, there is a *flat fare* between two points. If you are taking a cab for business purposes, you can ask the driver for a **receipt**. You then give the receipt to your company as a record of your expenses.

- It is customary to **tip** the **cab driver** (taxi driver) 15% of the fare.

Alternate Words

taxicab	taxi/cab .
taxi driver	cab driver
passenger	rider

Notes on E

Other forms of transportation are found throughout the country, but are not the customary means of transportation. **Monorails** may be used in airports or parks, as in the monorail around Disney World. **Streetcars** are used New Orleans, LA. An **aerial tramway** may connect an island with the mainland, as between Roosevelt Island and New York City (the island of Manhattan). San Francisco is unique in its use of **cable cars**. **Horse-drawn carriages** are used mostly for sightseeing, as in Charleston, SC.

Alternate Words

streetcars	trolleys

Suggested Activities

1. Have the students tell each other about any means of public transportation they have been on in this country. If they travel on buses regularly, ask them to tell each other which bus they take, where they catch it, where they get off, and how much the fare is.

2. Have the students tell a story about one of the people in each of the pictures (A through D), using the vocabulary listed and any additional words you have given.

56 Air Travel

Notes About the Dictionary Page	The woman on this page is traveling on business. Each frame follows her through the various steps of getting onto the plane.
Cross-Reference	*Aircraft (57)*

Alternate Words

baggage	luggage	**porter**	redcap/skycap
suitcase	bag	**ticket**	coupon
flight attendant	steward(ess)	**pilot**	captain

Notes on Scene 1

- The woman is checking her **garment bag** at the check-in counter.

- **Travelers** must check in at the terminal (57). Some terminals offer curbside check-in, where **baggage** (luggage) can be checked with the **porter** before entering the terminal. The porter may also carry the baggage into the terminal for the traveler. Passengers are allowed one **carry-on bag**, which must be able to fit under the seat.

- *Check-in counters* are for passengers who wish to purchase tickets or just check baggage. At the check-in counter, the passenger is checked in for the flight and assigned a seat. Seating may be in the smoking or nonsmoking section, near the window or on the **aisle**. The clerk issues a **boarding pass** and tells the passenger which *gate* to report to for departure.

Notes on Scene 2

- The woman is now placing her bag on the **conveyor belt** to be passed through the **x-ray screener.**

- Passengers must go through the security area before they can board the plane. Only passengers are admitted through **security**. All bags and coats must go through the screener. Certain items, such as cameras and film (100), can be hand-searched by the security guard.

Notes on the Inset

- On some flights, there may be a third person in the **cockpit**, the *flight engineer*. Otherwise there is just the **pilot** and **copilot**.

- Certain airlines allow passengers to visit the cockpit during flight. Others may provide cameras in the cockpit, so that passengers can view the takeoff and landing from the pilot's perspective.

Notes on Scene 3

- The woman is now showing the **flight attendant** her boarding pass.

- Passengers board at the gate and must surrender the airline ticket to the flight attendant. Upon boarding, the flight attendant shows the passenger where (which side of the plane) her seat is located. The passengers must stow away everything they carried on board, sit down, and fasten their seat belts (50).

Suggested Activities

1. Have the students tell a story about the woman traveler in the pictures, including where she is going and the steps she takes once she arrives at the airport.

2. Ask the students to describe any experiences they have had traveling by air in this country, using the vocabulary listed and any additional words you have given.

57 Aircraft

Cross-Reference	*Air Travel (56), Space (75)*

Alternate Words

jet plane	airplane
helicopter	chopper
blimp	dirigible/zeppelin
propeller plane	prop plane

Notes on A

Type of Aircraft	Distinguishing Features
hot air balloon	a balloon made of light material, such as silk or plastic, which contains hot air, usually heated by a burner, so that it expands and becomes lighter than the surrounding air; often has a car or gondola attached below for carrying passengers or scientific instruments
helicopter	sustained in the air by horizontally rotating blades (**rotor**) turning on vertical axes by virtue of power supplied by an engine; stabilized by a vertical rotor in the tail
private jet	a privately owned plane, usually with seating capacity of two to twelve
glider	an engineless, heavier-than-air craft for gliding from a higher to a lower level by the action of *gravity* or from a lower to higher level by the action of *air currents*
blimp	a lighter-than-air airship; filled with light gas, usually *helium*, which gives it buoyancy; often used for observation
hang glider	a very light glider with an open framework to which a person is strapped
propeller plane	an airplane moved by a *propeller,* a device having a rotating hub with radiating blades
jet plane	an airplane moved by *jet engines,* which produce forward motion by the rearward exhaust of a jet of fluid or heated air and gases

Notes on B

Before the **plane** takes off, it is refueled and checked for any mechanical problems. Baggage and other **cargo**, including live animals, are loaded into the **cargo area** of the plane. At the same time the passenger area is cleaned, and new food and supplies are brought on board.

Once all the passengers are on board the plane, the flight attendants prepare the plane for **takeoff**. Passengers are warned that seat belts (50) must be fastened, all seats must be in the upright position, all smoking materials must be extinguished, tray tables (56) must be raised, and carry-on bags (56) must be stowed in the overhead luggage compartment (56) or under the seat.

Planes must file a flight plan with the **control tower**. *Air traffic controllers* monitor the arrivals and departures of planes on radar screens. After the plane has taxied to the runway, it must be cleared for takeoff by an air traffic controller.

When the plane reaches *cruising altitude,* the pilot turns off the "Fasten Seat Belt" sign and allows the passengers to move about the cabin. If there is *turbulence,* the pilot will turn the "Fasten Seat Belt" sign on.

The plane begins its *descent* 30 to 45 minutes before it gets to its destination. The landing gear is lowered during the final landing *approach*. When the plane begins its approach to the airport, the passengers must adhere to the same rules as on takeoff. Once the plane touches down, passengers may not get up until the plane has come to a complete stop at the **terminal**.

After the plane has arrived, the passengers go to the *baggage claim area* to get their bags.

Suggested Activities	1. Have the students bring in a picture of a plane from a magazine and label the parts of the plane (items 8–15).
	2. Have the students pick out one of the types of aircraft illustrated and tell a story about its occupant(s).

58 In Port

Cross-Reference

Boating (59)

Alternate Words

pier	dock/wharf	**gangway**	gangplank
port	seaport/harbor	**ocean liner**	cruise ship

Usage Notes

The size of the vessel determines whether it is considered a boat or a ship; **ferries**, **tugboats**, and dinghies (59) are boats, while **ocean liners**, **tankers**, and aircraft carriers (48) are ships.

Culture Notes

- **Ports** are usually centers of industry and population. Since the United States was settled during the time when shipping was a major means of transportation, most large cities were originally port settlements. Today *shipping* remains an important part of the economic structure of these cities.

- The largest ports in the United States are: New York; New Orleans; Houston; Valdez, AL; Baton Rouge; Tampa; Norfolk; Corpus Christi; Long Beach; and Baltimore. Other well-known ports are: San Francisco; Seattle; Miami; San Diego; and Newport, RI.

Resource Notes

bow	the front of a ship
stern	the back of a ship
windlass	the device for raising or hauling objects; in the illustration, the windlass is used to hoist and drop the **anchor**
bollard	a thick, low post on a wharf to which mooring lines are attached
line	rope
lighthouse	a structure that sends out a light to guide sailors
starboard	the right side of a ship
port	the left side of a ship
bridge	the raised platform from which the ship is navigated
longshoreman	a person employed on the wharves to load and unload vessels

Kind of Vessel	Distinguishing Features
containership	a ship built to hold cargo packed in uniform, sealed **containers**
barge	a flat-bottomed vessel meant to be pushed or towed, used for transporting *freight* or passengers
tugboat	a small, powerful boat for towing or pushing larger vessels
tanker	a ship designed to carry oil or other liquids
tall ship	a restored, old, multimasted sailing vessel used for training and display
trawler	a fishing boat that uses a trawl (fishing) net

Suggested Activities

1. Have the students ask each other questions about this vocabulary using questions beginning with "Which vessel?" such as, "Which vessel pushes other boats?"

2. Have the students choose one of the ships on which they would like to take an imaginary trip. They then tell the other students about the trip, including where they went, for how long, for what purpose, etc.

59 Pleasure Boating

Notes About the Dictionary Page

This page depicts a dock/boating area, most likely on a lake or inlet.

Cross-Reference

Port (58), Beach (90–91)

Resource Notes

Water safety: Boaters and waterskiers should always wear **life jackets** (life vests) (89). Boats that are powered by human energy (**windsurfers, water-skiers**, and **sailboats** using their sails) have right of way over **motorboats**. There are no licenses for operators of boats. Drinking and boating is the equivalent of drinking and driving. It is always wise to use the *buddy system* for water sports.

Kind of Boat	Distinguishing Features
canoe	propelled by **paddles**; constructed of aluminum, wood, fiberglass, or plastic; seats two to four people; originated by the American Indians; outside of the United States, it is called a North American canoe
sailboat	can be a small, one-person boat, or a large, multimasted vessel, may have an auxiliary (engine); a **rudder** is a vertical device, controlled by the *tiller*, that turns the boat; sailboats may have either a *keel* or a **centerboard**: a keel is a projection under the *hull* that can be filled with ballast and keeps the boat from sideslipping or tilting, while a centerboard is a board that can be inserted through a slit in the hull to keep the boat from side-slipping but that can be pulled up so the boat can sail in shallow water; the **mast** is the vertical pole that supports the sail and **boom**; the boom is horizontal and swings back and forth to allow the sail to be at different angles to the wind
motorboat	propelled by an outboard or inboard engine; may be designed for racing (powerboat, speedboat, cigarette)
sailboard	a board to which a rotating sail is attached for *windsurfing* (windsailing)

cabin cruiser	a motorboat with living quarters (the cabin)
kayak	propelled by a double-bladed paddle; originated by the Eskimos; seats one or two people; outside of the United States, called a canoe
dinghy	an auxiliary boat to a larger vessel; rowed, sailed, or motorized
inflatable raft	made of light or heavy rubber; may or may not have an engine
rowboat	propelled by **oars** that are secured in **oarlocks**; usually rowed by one person
catamaran	equipped with a sail; has two pontoons and a deck
shell	a light, narrow boat used for racing; also called a scull; propelled with oars by one or more people; as a sport, called crew

Suggested Activities

1. Have one student point to a picture of a boat or piece of equipment and the other students name it.

2. Have the students pick out one of the pleasure crafts that have people in it and tell a story about the boaters, using the vocabulary listed and any additional words you have given.

3. Have each student describe what kind of pleasure boat or equipment he/she would like to own and why.

60 & 61 Plants and Trees

Cross-Reference

Foods (6–9, 14–18), Seasonal Verbs (26)

Notes on Flowers

- Homeowners take pride in their *front lawns, backyards,* and *gardens.* Some grow vegetables and herbs (8–9), but most grow flowers, usually as borders, planted with a variety of *perennials* that bloom from early spring to late fall. Perennials are flowers that bloom once a year for many years, and are contrasted with annuals, which last only one growing season.

- You go to a local *flower shop* (florist) to buy *cut flowers.* Flowers are given as a token of romantic love, as a gift from a dinner guest to a host, as a get-well wish for a hospital patient, and as an apology. People often give flowers, mostly to women, on special occasions, such as birthdays and wedding anniversaries. Florists do their biggest business on Valentine's Day and Mother's Day. *Corsages* are given to women when they are guests of honor; young women often get corsages from their escorts on prom night.

  Flowers may be sent to the family of someone who has died to be displayed at the wake and on the funeral car, but this will depend on the religion and wishes of the deceased. Similarly, religious customs will determine whether flowers are placed on the grave.

- At large formal parties, flowers are used as decorations and for table *centerpieces*. At weddings, the bride carries a *bouquet*, usually of all white flowers; the groom wears a *boutonniere* on his lapel, usually of Stephanotis; and the *flower girl* scatters flower petals along the aisle before the bride walks down it. After the ceremony, the bride tosses her bouquet to the single, female guests; the one who catches it is supposed to be the next to get married.

- Many flowers, such as lilies and chrysanthemums, have hundreds of varieties. A few of each flower's distinguishing features are listed below:

Flower	*Distinguishing Features*
tulips	grown from **bulbs**; come in many heights and colors; are associated with Holland (the Netherlands); a Darwin tulip is illustrated; tulip breeding is a profession, and certain bulbs can cost thousands of dollars
pansies	have numerous colors and combinations that often lead to amazingly human expressions
lilies	grown from bulbs; the most common varieties are tiger lilies (pictured), day lilies, and Easter lilies
(chrysanthe)mums	originally from China; its varieties are named for the shapes and arrangements of their blossom **petals**, such as incurved (pictured), spoon, anemone, and pompom; associated with the autumn
daisies	really English, or true, daisies, since other daisies, like shasta daisies, are chrysanthemums; we say "fresh as a daisy"
marigolds	can be six-inch plants to four-foot plants; the two original varieties are French marigolds (pictured) and African marigolds
petunias	easy to grow; can tolerate chilly to hot weather, any kind of soil, shade as well as sunshine
daffodils	grown from bulbs; a type of narcissus; immortalized in a poem, "I Wandered Lonely as a Cloud…," by William Wordsworth
crocuses	grown from bulbs; considered harbingers of spring
hyacinths	grown from bulbs; name comes from a Greek myth; produced in great numbers in the Netherlands
irises	more than 20,000 varieties; named by the ancient Greeks, "iris" means "rainbow"; the model for the fleur-de-lis, a heraldic emblem; the tall bearded iris is illustrated
orchids	originate in the *jungles* of tropical and subtropical regions; are very delicate and often used for corsages and bouquets
zinnias	a great variety of colors, contours, and sizes, from one-footers with flowers the size of coat buttons to three-foot flowers with six-inch flowers; there are two variations in the pronunciation of zinnia [zĭn' yə/zĭn' ē ə], and both are acceptable in American English

gardenias	white, sweet-smelling flowers that are popular as corsages
poinsettias	green and red (or green and white) plants associated with the Christmas season; the red (or white) part of the plant is the upper leaves, which are narrower than the green ones lower down
violets	with pansies, are part of the viola family
buttercups	grow wild in spring fields and meadows; cultivated, they are known as Ranunculus
roses	there are over 5,000 recognized species and varieties of roses; most are fragrant and bloom in June; the favorite type for garden-bed planting is the hybrid tea (illustrated); each shade of rose is said to carry a meaning, such as the red rose symbolizing love
sunflowers	may grow to 12 feet in height; grown commercially for the highly nutritious *seeds* formed in the center of the flower and for the oil that they contain; Vincent Van Gogh painted "Sunflowers"

Notes on Grasses and Grains

- **Sugarcane** is one of several sources of sugar, the others being sugar beets, sugar maple, sorghum, and sugar palm. The *granulated sugar* we buy is most often derived from sugarcane. People use sugar in coffee and tea. Sugar is one of the main ingredients in ice cream, candy, soft drinks, cakes, cookies, and other pastries.

- **Rice, wheat, oats** and **corn** are staples in our diet. With potatoes (7), they provide the complex carbohydrates from which our bodies derive energy and the fiber we need for good digestion. We eat breads made of wheat, rye, and oat bran; crackers made of wheat, rye, and rice; cereals made of rice, wheat, oats, and corn; and noodles made of wheat (and sometimes rice). Kernel corn and corn on the cob are eaten as vegetables (6). Oats, corn, *barley*, and other grains are used as *feed* for livestock.

- While the other grasses and grains are grown domestically, we import most of our rice and sugarcane.

Notes on Trees and Other Plants — There are two kinds of trees: *evergreens*, which have leaves that remain on the tree for more than one to many years, and *deciduous trees*, which have large spreading leaves that are shed each autumn. Like flowers, different trees grow in different climates and conditions.

Tree	*Distinguishing Features*
redwood	giant *sequoia* and redwood trees are evergreens found mainly in California; commonly grow 200 to 275 feet tall and are 8 to 10 feet in diameter; the General Sherman Tree in Sequoia National Park is 272 feet tall, has an average basal diameter of 30.7 feet, and is estimated to be 3,800 years old
palm	native North American palm trees are grown in warm parts of the country, such as southern California, Florida, and Hawaii; there are two groups of palms: fan palms and feather palms
eucalyptus	an evergreen native to Australia that is found in California

dogwood	deciduous trees that grow to about 25 to 30 feet; different varieties are found throughout the country; well known for its beautiful flowers
magnolia	have either evergreen or deciduous leaves and usually white, yellow, rose, or purple flowers appearing in early spring, often before the leaves; they attain a height of 60 to 90 feet and are found mostly in the southeastern states
poplar	deciduous trees, native to North America, that sometimes reach a height of over 100 feet; when ripe, their fruit splits open and releases many tiny, dark-brown seeds; each seed is attached to a tuft of cottony hairs and is blown by the wind
willow	the willow family includes willows, poplars or cottonwoods, and aspens; willows are found throughout the country; many are shrubs, but some are trees; the *weeping willow* and *pussy willow* are well-known species
birch	deciduous; many varieties have distinctive white bark; small to medium-sized trees, growing to about 80 feet; found in most parts of the country; the twigs of some species are distilled to get oil of wintergreen
oak	found throughout the country; some are deciduous, and some evergreen; they grow to a maximum of 150 feet; North American oaks are divided into two groups: white oaks and red oaks; chestnut oaks are a subsection of the white oak group; the willow oaks and live oaks are subsections of the red oak group; we speak of "the mighty oak"; the expression, "The **acorn** never falls far from its tree," is something akin to "like father, like son"
pine	evergreens; its leaves are **needles**, which are usually in bundles of two to five; they are *conifers*, with **cones** whose scales may or may not have prickles; found on the West Coast, East Coast, in the Lake States, and Southeast; sometimes grow to over 200 feet
elm	found in the eastern half of the country; they grow to a maximum height of 130 feet
holly	evergreen trees or shrubs that produce red fruit (**berries**); found in the South and on the Eastern seaboard; the foliage is used for a Christmas decoration, as in the Christmas carol, "Deck the halls with boughs of holly. . ."
maple	found mostly in the eastern half of the country; they have deciduous leaves and reach a maximum height of 130 feet; they have distinctive paired winged seeds, which kids like to split and put on their noses
cactus	cacti (also cactuses, cactus) are found in the Southeast, Southwest, and southern California; they are considered desert plants; they do not have leaves, except for *spines*, and some have single colorful flowers
Notes on Poisonous Plants	**Poisonous plants** produce irritating oils that cause itchy skin rashes at the place of contact. The rash can spread over the body through touch. Most people can control the itching with over-the-counter remedies. Some people have severe allergic reactions to poisonous plants and have to be very careful to avoid them.

Suggested Activities

1. Have as many live flowers as possible brought into class. (You may be able to get donations of a few flowers from various local florists.) Have the students identify the live flowers from the pictures. Then have them ask each other questions beginning with "Which flower?" such as, "Which flower is yellow, has five small petals on the bottom and five long petals like a bell in the middle?"

2. Have the students pair off and tell each other which grains they eat at breakfast, lunch, and dinner. For example, "I eat hot oatmeal for breakfast. I have a sandwich for lunch on whole wheat bread. For dinner, I have rice. . ." Have the students report to the rest of the class what grains their classmates eat.

3. Bring in a copy of the Joyce Kilmer poem, "Trees." Have the students read and understand the poem and recite it either as a group or individually.

4. If it is feasible, arrange a field trip for the students to a nearby arboretum or botanic garden.

5. Have the students learn the characteristics of poisonous plants. Then have them discuss possible treatments with you, using vocabulary from the Medical pages (39–41).

62 Simple Animals

Cross-Reference   *Animals (63–69), Beach (90–91)*

Language Notes   Some of the plural forms of the simple animals are unusual, or can be formed in different ways:

squid	squid/squids
octopus	octopuses/octopi
starfish	starfish/starfishes
shrimp	shrimp/shrimps

Resource Notes   The animal kingdom is divided into 17 branches, or phyla. Each branch is further divided into classes. The branch is indicated for each of the animals pictured as the first item under the distinguishing features column.

Animal	*Distinguishing Features*
snail	mollusk; snails are both marine and terrestrial animals; they have hard, spiral shells; snails are considered delicacies by some (in French, called *escargots*)
oyster	mollusk; they fasten themselves to the stones and rocks of ocean shallows; popular as a food (eaten raw on the half-shell or cooked) and considered an aphrodisiac; they are a source of pearls
mussel	mollusk; long hairs attach the sea mussel to its rock; sea mussels are fished from temperate waters and eaten, mostly in stews; the shell of the freshwater mussel is used for *mother-of-pearl* buttons

slug   mollusk; slugs are similar to snails but have no shells and are land animals; they are found in gardens where they often become pests; we use the word "sluggish" to describe someone who moves slowly

squid   mollusk; they are marine animals used as bait and food

octopus   mollusk; octopi have eight arms, called **tentacles**; they can change their colors to camouflage themselves; they also can squirt brown ink to protect themselves; can be used as food

starfish   spiny-skinned animals; they feed on bivalve mollusks; if they are broken in two, starfish regenerate into two new starfish over time

shrimp   joint-legged animals, crustacean class; they swim backwards with the aid of their fantails; shrimps are popular as food; the word "shrimp" is used disparagingly or affectionately to refer to a small person or thing

crab   joint-legged animals, crustacean class; most crabs are sea creatures; they have five pairs of legs and the front pair end in *pincers*; there are many different varieties of crabs that are popular as food; a grumpy, irritable person is a "crabby" person

scallop   mollusk; the part of the scallop that is eaten is the large white muscle of the animal inside the shell; the shells of scallops are often used decoratively

worm   segmented worms; worms are land animals used as bait in fishing; worms are part of birds' diets; the expression "the early bird catches the worm" means the one who gets there first profits

jellyfish   sac-like animals; jellyfish have translucent bodies and stinging tentacles on their undersides

lobster   joint-legged animals, crustacean class; lobsters have hard shells, claws, pincers, feelers, and a tail; they are delicacies; the lobster pictured is a Maine lobster

Suggested Activities

1. Have the students list the animals on this page in one column. In the next column, they should put a check mark next to all the animals that people eat. In the last column, they should put a check mark next to all the animals they eat. You may ask the students to tell each other how the animals they eat are prepared.

2. Have the students take turns asking each other questions about the animals on this page, beginning with "Which animal?" such as, "Which animal has eight tentacles and changes colors?"

63 Insects

Notes About the Dictionary Page	All the animals on this page belong to the branch of animals known as joint-legged animals. They all belong to the insect class except scorpions and spiders, which are arachnids, and centipedes, which are jaw-footed animals.
Cross-Reference	*Animals (62, 64–69)*
Supplemental Vocabulary	fly; crawl; bite

Alternate Words

mantis	praying mantis/praying mantid
cockroach	roach
ladybug	ladybird/lady beetle
firefly	lightning bug/glowworm

Culture and Resource Notes

The different **insects** on this page prompt a variety of reactions from us. We take many measures to protect against these pests. We put screens on our windows to keep out flying insects. We spray and put *insect traps* out to control roaches and ants. We get *exterminators* for termites and carpenter ants. We get *fly strips*, *flyswatters*, "zappers," and lanterns to keep flies away. We coat ourselves with *insect repellent* when we go out in the woods in the summer. We spray vegetation, and we put *mothballs* among the old clothes in the attic. Most of these actions are based on our fear of being stung or hurt by these insects or because they multiply rapidly.

Insect	*Distinguishing Features*
caterpillar	forms a **cocoon** about itself from which it emerges as a **butterfly**, which has beautiful, broad, various-shaped wings, often with striking colors and patterns
dragonfly	also called a darning needle because of the shape of its body; it is harmless to us, but feeds on **flies**, *gnats*, and **mosquitoes**, and is often near ponds and lakes
cricket	makes a distinctive chirping sound in summer; Jiminy Cricket is the popular Disney cartoon character in *Pinocchio*; the cricket's relative, the **grasshopper**, is green and difficult to see in the grass, has a distinctive hopping motion, and can be quite destructive to plant life
mantis	also called the praying mantis because it clasps its prey in its forelimbs and holds its forelimbs up as if in prayer; it is harmless to us and some say that it is bad luck to kill a praying mantis; the female praying mantis sometimes devours her mate after he has wooed her; the mantis is valued by farmers because it eats pest insects
scorpion	is feared because of its **sting**, which can be toxic or poisonous; the scorpion's tail is often coiled over its back
cockroach	can infest our homes, especially urban apartments; roaches are hard to destroy and multiply incredibly fast
termite	eats wood, including the structures of houses

ant	there are several kinds of ants: carpenter ants, like termites, eat wood and create problems for homeowners; red ants can inflict terrible bites on people; black ants can be a nuisance at cookouts and picnics
fly	is mostly a nuisance, but some kinds can bite
mosquito	not only bites, leaving an itchy swelling behind, but it also carries diseases, the worst of these being *malaria* in certain parts of the world
beetle	some kinds can destroy vegetation; over 300,000 species
moth	circles around streetlights on summer nights; can eat holes into clothing; "like a moth to a flame" is used to describe someone who is irresistably attracted to someone else
ladybug	thought to be good luck if one lands on you; is really a kind of beetle; there is a well-known Mother Goose rhyme about the ladybug: Ladybird, Ladybird, fly away home!/Your house is on fire, your children all gone,/All but one, and her name is Ann,/And she crept under the pudding pan.
spider	is not generally popular, but it feeds on insects that could otherwise multiply and literally desolate the Earth; it spins incredible **webs** in which it ensnares its prey; most spiders are harmless to us; a few, including the "black widow," have a strong poison that is very potent, but that is seldom fatal because of the small quantity produced
firefly	children love to catch fireflies in the summer twilight and watch them glow in the dark; fireflies are really a kind of beetle that are found in many different parts of the world
bee	like a **wasp**, it can inflict painful stings; some people have allergic reactions that make these stings potentially fatal; bees carry *pollen* from flower to flower, thus playing an important role in flower reproduction; they produce *honey* in their *hives*; "the birds and the bees" is a synonym for "the facts of life"; "busy as a bee" is a common expression
centipede	has 100 pairs of legs (actually, adult centipedes have from 15 to 173 pairs of legs); its first pair of legs forms poison claws, which can paralyze worms and insects and sometimes sicken people

Suggested Activities

1. Have the students categorize the insects above into two categories: insects which are harmful to us and those which are harmless.

2. Have the students ask each other questions about insects using questions beginning with "Which insect?" such as, "Which insect has a tail coiled over its back?"

64 Birds

Meat (10–11), Animals (63, 65–69), Farm (81)

Usage Notes
- Many of the birds listed are used to convey something either symbolic or allegorical. For example, "chicken" and "turkey" have other meanings when calling a person by either of these names. Politically, "a hawk" has come to mean someone in favor of war; "a dove" opposed. Other such names you may want to introduce are: stool pigeon, lame duck, old crow, night owl.

- The **rooster** gives a loud crow when the sun rises, and daybreak is also called "cock's crow." A person who "crows" is boasting or expressing pleasure.

- The **parrot** is known for its ability to mimic voices, and to "parrot" someone is to imitate them.

Culture Notes
- *Birdwatching* is a hobby. *Bird sanctuaries* are public areas kept to protect birds from natural and human predators. Zoos (87) often have bird houses.

- There are several kinds of birds that are nearly extinct and classified as *endangered species*, such as bald eagles and condors. It is illegal to kill or harm these species.

- Some of the singing/talking birds on this page, such as the **canary, parakeet,** and parrot, are kept as pets. Some of the birds pictured, such as the **pheasant, turkey, chicken, duck,** and **goose,** are used as food.

- Some, but far from all, of the birds listed are used for names of professional *sports teams.* Baseball: St. Louis Cardinals, Toronto Blue Jays; Football: Seattle SeaHawks, Philadelphia Eagles; Hockey: Pittsburgh Penguins (see Appendix E).

Resource Notes
The animal kingdom is divided into 17 branches, or phyla. Each branch is further divided into classes, which is subdivided into orders. All birds belong to the branch known as the Spinal-Cord (Vertebrate) Animals, Bird Class. The orders for most of the birds illustrated on this page are given as the first item under the distinguishing features column.

Bird	*Distinguishing Features*
pigeon	dove-like birds; pigeons are city birds; people often feed bread crumbs or peanuts to the pigeons in the parks; people train certain types of pigeons, such as homing pigeons; a *dove* is a type of pigeon and is the symbol of peace
hummingbird	hummingbirds and swifts; very small birds; the male has brilliant iridescent plumage; they have slender **bills** and a very extensile tongue
crow	perching birds; black, glossy birds; noted for their alertness and intelligence
sea gull	shorebirds and gulls; aquatic birds that usually remain near shore; important harbor scavengers; usually white and gray in color
eagle	daytime hunters; birds of prey noted for their strength, size, grace, keenness of vision, and powers of flight; the figure of a bald eagle with **wings** extended is the national bird and is pictured on the coat of arms of the United States; a person with "eagle eyes" has sharp, clear vision

owl	night hunters; birds of prey noted for their large head, large, almost forwardly directed eyes, and short, hooked bill; associated with the sound "whoo"; we say someone is "wise as an owl"
hawk	daytime hunters; birds of prey with very keen eyes; we use the expression "to watch (someone) like a hawk"
blue jay	perching birds; found in eastern North America; has a handsome crest; plumage of the upper parts mainly bright blue
robin	perching birds; found throughout North America; has a red breast; known as spring's harbinger
sparrow	perching birds; many different sparrows; the English sparrow is prevalent in cities and nests almost anywhere
cardinal	perching birds; the male cardinal is one of the most beautiful of North American birds, wearing the red hat of the official of the church for whom it was named
ostrich	ostriches; swift-footed, flightless birds; according to popular belief, when pursued, ostriches hide their heads in the sand and believe they can't be seen
woodpecker	woodpeckers; climb and rest on trees; with their very hard bills, they drill the bark or wood of trees for insect food; Woody Woodpecker is a famous cartoon character
peacock	chicken-like birds; peacocks are male peafowls; they have tail **feathers** they spread at will into breathtakingly beautiful fans, with iridescent colors ; we say someone is "proud as a peacock"
pelican	fully webbed birds; have very large bills and distensible pouches in which fish are caught; often perch on posts on piers
penguin	wedge-winged birds; short-legged aquatic birds; found near Antarctica, the Falkland Islands, and New Zealand; many different species, Adelie pictured; they stand erect but walk clumsily and have wings that resemble flippers, which are used for swimming; they cannot fly; their black-and-white plumage resembles tuxedos
swan	goose-like birds; have heavy bodies and long, elegant necks; aquatic birds that walk awkwardly, fly strongly, and swim gracefully; their plumage is usually pure white when they are adults; it is thought that before dying a swan sings a beautiful lament; we refer to someone's last public appearance as their "swansong"
flamingo	stork-like birds; flamingos range in color from pale pink to bright scarlet, depending on their diet; aquatic birds, they have swanlike necks and strong bills; Florida is well known for its flamingos
stork	stork-like birds; wading birds with long, stout bills; storks are associated with the birth of children because of the nursery story that children are brought into the world by storks
roadrunner	cuckoo-like birds; is noted for running with great speed; is found from California to Mexico and eastward to Texas; also called chaparral bird; the Road Runner is a favorite cartoon character

Suggested Activities	1. Have the students organize the birds above into three categories: birds that are pets, birds that are used as food, and birds in nature.
	2. Have the students ask each other questions about birds using questions beginning with "Which bird?" such as, "Which bird looks like it is wearing a tuxedo?"

65 Fish and Reptiles

Cross-Reference	*Animals (63–64, 66–69), Outdoor Activities (88–89)*
Culture Notes	*Aquariums* are public exhibits of fish, amphibians, and reptiles. Zoos (87) often have reptile houses.
Resource Notes	The animal kingdom is divided into 17 branches, or phyla. All fish, amphibians, and reptiles belong to the branch known as the Spinal-Cord (Vertebrate) Animals.
Notes on A	A **fish** is a cold-blooded animal that lives in water. They breathe through **gills** to get oxygen. **Fins** are used for balance and for changing direction.

Fish	*Distinguishing Features*
sea horse	small fish whose head and forepart are flexed and resemble the head and neck of a horse
trout	a game fish usually found in lakes and streams, though some kinds of trout live in the sea; trout fishing is a popular sport
swordfish	the swordfish's sword is actually an extension of its upper jaw
eel	a long, snakelike fish with smooth, slimy skin
shark	spends its entire life searching for food; has an incredibly keen sense of smell and is acutely sensitive to vibrations in water; may attack people
stingray	has one or more large, sharp, barbed dorsal spines near the base of its whiplike tail, which is capable of inflicting severe wounds
flounder	the adult has both eyes on the same side of its head

Notes on B	A **reptile** is a cold-blooded animal that lays eggs on land. Young reptiles can breathe air. An **amphibian** is a cold-blooded animal that lives in water when young and on land as adults; they are born with gills that develop into lungs.

Reptile	*Distinguishing Features*
alligator	amphibian; similar to the *crocodile* except the upper teeth cover the lower, while a crocodile has a large lower tooth on each side, visible when the mouth is shut; alligator skin is used commercially for shoes and handbags, found around the Okefenokee Swamp in Georgia, the bayous in Louisiana, and the marshlands in Florida; "see ya' later, alligator" is an expression used to say good-bye

(garter) snake	reptile; the best known, most common, and most widely distributed of all North American snakes; it is harmless and identifiable by its long stripes and brilliant colors
rattlesnake	reptile; has a *rattle* made of a series of horny interlocking parts at the end of its tail, which it shakes to ward off its enemies; has a venomous bite that is poisonous and sometimes fatal
cobra	reptile; native to India and Africa; when excited, it flattens its head into a hood by expanding its ribs; cobra bites are very deadly; it can also squirt its *venom* into the eyes of its adversary, sometimes causing blindness in humans; it is deaf and cannot hear the music of the snake charmer, but it sways back and forth to the motion of the musician moving in time to the music
turtle	reptile; pet box turtles can live outdoors all summer and in winter will either hibernate under the soil or can be kept indoors, as long as the temperature is kept at 80°F during the day for them; we use the expression "slow as a turtle" to describe someone who is slow moving
iguana	reptile; desert iguanas, which are about a foot long, are found in United States; green iguanas, which grow to about three feet and have whiplike tails, are found in Central and South America; green iguanas usually live in trees near rivers and lakes and feed on leaves, fruit, and birds
salamander	amphibian; lizard-shaped; some species have lungs, some have gills, and others breathe through their skin; according to ancient folklore, is immune to fire
lizard	reptile; has dry, scaly skin; loves the sun and hibernates; if a lizard's tail is broken off, a new one grows; some fly, some walk on ceilings, some run on hind legs
frog	amphibian; it lives on land near creeks and ponds and hibernates; each spring, it must lay eggs in the water; **tadpoles** hatch from eggs and transform in stages into frogs or toads; frogs are tailless, with hind legs adapted for jumping, bulging eyes to spy prey and see danger, and darting, sticky tongues for catching food
tortoise	reptile; turtle and tortoise are unscientific names; the word "turtle" normally means all such animals, both aquatic and terrestrial, while the word "tortoise" normally means "land turtle"; tortoiseshell, however, comes from the hawksbill turtle, which lives in the sea; "The Tortoise and the Hare" is a popular fable (hare is a type of rabbit)

Suggested Activities	1. Write each of the animals on a separate index card and write the three categories (fish, amphibians, and reptiles) on large cards. Put the three category cards in three distinct places in the room. Have the students take turns picking an animal card and placing it with the correct category card.
	2. Have the students ask each other questions about fish, amphibians, and reptiles using questions beginning with "Which animal?" such as, "Which animal has two eyes on the same side of its head?"

66–69 Mammals I and II

Cross-Reference *Animals (62–65), Farming (81)*

Usage Notes
- "To ape" means "to mimic."

- We use similes having to do with the characteristics of animals, as in the following examples:

  as playful as a puppy   as blind as a bat   as strong as an ox
  as quiet as a mouse   as big as an elephant   as gentle as a lamb
  as stubborn as a mule   as sly as a fox   as hungry as a bear

- We also use epithets, such as "eager beaver" and "filthy pig," to refer to people.

Culture Notes
- Zoos (87) are centers for the research and study of animals, where people can go to observe the animals and can sometimes feed them. Some zoos have the animals in environments that resemble their natural habitats. Aquatic mammals can be seen at *aquariums*. Some aquariums have live performances of trained **seals** and **dolphins**.

- Several mammals are nearly extinct and classified as *endangered species*, such as **bisons** and **pandas**. It is illegal to kill or harm these species.

- Many children's stories have animals as main characters, such as "The Three Little Pigs," "Little Red Riding Hood," and "Goldilocks and the Three Bears." Nursery rhymes also often revolve around animals, such as "Mary Had a Little Lamb," "Baa, Baa, Black Sheep," and "Little Miss Muffet."

- As with the birds, some mammals are used for names of professional *sports teams*. Baseball: Detroit Tigers, Chicago Cubs; Football: Detroit Lions, Miami Dolphins, and Chicago Bears (see Appendix E).

Resource Notes
The animal kingdom is divided into 17 branches, or phyla. Each branch is further divided into classes. All of the animals pictured belong to the branch of Spinal-Cord (Vertebrate) Animals, Mammal Class, which is further subdivided into orders. The order for each of the animals pictured is given below.

Notes on Pouched, Toothless, or Flying Mammals

koala   pouched mammal (marsupial); native to Australia (70); has soft fur and a lovable nature; carries its babies in a **pouch**; lives in trees and eats only a certain kind of eucalyptus leaf (61)

armadillo   toothless mammal; armed with bony plates; prowls at night; found in Florida, Texas, Arizona, and southward to Brazil; if frightened, it rolls itself into an impenetrable ball

kangaroo   pouched mammal; found only in Australia; is the national symbol of Australia; its **tail** is used as a support and in balancing; full grown, it commonly weighs 200 pounds and stands about five feet tall; newborn, it is less than an inch long; the baby (called a "joey") makes its way into the pouch, where the mother pumps milk into it; by about four months, it has fur and peeks out of the pouch, looking much the way most pictures show mother and baby

bat	claw-winged mammal; has wings and is the only mammal capable of true flight; has a thumb and toes with claws by which it suspends itself, often head downward, when at rest; is a *nocturnal* animal; some feed on insects, some on fruit, and some suck the blood of other mammals; someone insane is said to have "bats in his belfry"
anteater	toothless mammal; there are several varieties; it is tube-headed and has no teeth; has a mouth so small that a person cannot get his finger in, but it has a two-foot long tongue that whips out to snare a meal; when attacked, it slashes with strong claws developed to tear open anthills; found in Central and tropical South America

Notes on Rodents

chipmunk	gnawing mammal; found throughout North America (70); ground-dwelling squirrel with a striped back; from April to October it runs through forests and brushy areas gathering food, some of which it stores in cheek pockets and buries underground for winter; it utters several rapid "chips" and a long trill when startled
rat	gnawing mammal; considerably larger than a mouse, and with different teeth features; some forms live around human habitations and in ships; are destructive pests, consuming great quantities of food and transmitting various diseases, the most infamous of which was *bubonic plague* (the Black Death)
gopher	gnawing mammal; found in North and Central America; a burrowing rodent the size of a large rat; has small eyes, short ears, strong claws on the forelimbs, and large cheek pouches
mouse	gnawing mammal; lives everywhere except a few Pacific islands; the city mouse has large eyes, ears, and long whiskers, designed for prying into crevices and behind walls; the country mouse (field, wood, and pine mouse) is food for every animal of prey; Mickey Mouse is one of Disney's most famous cartoon characters
squirrel	gnawing mammal; small to medium-sized; has a bushy tail and long, strong hind limbs that allow it to leap from branch to branch; it feeds largely on nuts and seeds, which it stores for winter
porcupine	gnawing mammal; relatively large; has stiff, sharp, erect bristles, or **quills**, mingled with the hair of its coat for defending itself
beaver	gnawing mammal; semiaquatic, it has webbed hind feet and a broad flat tail; it feeds mainly on bark and twigs; is known for its building of dams (80)
rabbit	leaping mammal; not technically a rodent, but has rodent-like characteristics; moves in hops, at times with great speed; can be kept as a pet; is associated with the Easter holiday (Easter Bunny); Bugs Bunny is a famous cartoon character

Notes on Hoofed Mammals

hippopotamus	even-toed, hoofed mammal; plural, hippopotami; is a large herb eater; has an extremely large head and mouth, bare, very thick skin, and short legs; its name means "river horse" in Greek, and it is commonly seen on the rivers of Africa (70); the name is often shortened to "hippo"

llama	even-toed, hoofed mammal; belongs to the camel family but without a hump; famous beast of burden of South America (70), it can travel 20 miles a day with a heavy load; is stubborn and temperamental
rhinoceros	odd-toed, hoofed mammal; found in Africa and Asia (70); is a large, powerful herb eater; has one or two heavy upright **horns** on the snout; the name is often shortened to "rhino," from the Latin word for "nose"
elephant	trunk-nosed mammal; found in Africa and Asia; is a very large, nearly hairless herb eater; the snout is prolonged into a muscular **trunk**; two incisors in the upper jaw (especially in the male) develop into long curved **tusks** that supply *ivory*
zebra	odd-toed, hoofed mammal; is a bad-tempered and stubborn member of the horse family; its stripes serve as *camouflage* in the shades of trees; most roam the plains of Africa; they live in bands led by a stallion
bison	even-toed, hoofed mammal; commonly misnomered "buffalo"; nearly extinct in North America and is found only on preserves
pony	odd-toed, hoofed mammal; is a small horse, usually not more than 14 hands high
horse (81)	odd-toed, hoofed mammal; is known as a work animal, a racing animal, and a sport animal; its height is measured in hands and its age can be told by examining its teeth; an adult female is a *mare*; an adult male capable of reproducing is a *stallion*; a castrated adult male is a *gelding*; a **foal** is a young horse that is not yet one year old; a *colt* is a young male of not more than four years; a *filly* is a young female of not more than four years
donkey	odd-toed, hoofed mammal; a domestic *ass*; smaller than a horse with long ears; sure-footed beast of burden known for its stubbornness
sheep (81)	even-toed, hoofed mammal; a relative of the goat; its coat is sheared and made into *wool*; it is raised in a *flock* that is tended by a *shepherd*; a **lamb** is a young sheep, less than a year old or with no permanent teeth; someone "sheepish" is meek
deer	even-toed, hoofed mammal; it bounds gracefully through woodland meadows; the mule deer, black-tailed deer, and white-tailed deer inhabit North America; the male (*buck*) usually has **antlers**; the female is called a *doe*; deer are often hunted; its meat is called *venison*; mating is in the fall, and **fawns**, born in the spring, stay with their mothers all summer
goat	even-toed, hoofed mammal; member of the cattle or oxen family; male usually has horns and a beard; feeds on almost anything except tin cans; some kinds of goats provide milk for goat's milk cheeses; angora and cashmere wool come from particular long-haired goats; the young goat is called a *kid*
giraffe	even-toed, hoofed mammal; a tall, long-necked, spotted, cud-chewing mammal of Africa; it is the tallest living four-footed animal
hog	even-toed, hoofed mammal; a domesticated *swine* weighing more than 120 pounds (a *pig* weighs less than 120 pounds) raised for market; a *sow* is an adult female; a *boar* is an uncastrated adult male

cow (81)   even-toed, hoofed mammal; the adult female of a bovine animal; it chews its *cud*, the portion of food that goes from the first stomach to its mouth to be chewed a second time; the **bull** is the adult uncastrated male; the **calf** is the young animal

camel   even-toed, hoofed mammal; there are two kinds of camels, the Bactrian (illustrated), which has two **humps** and long, shaggy hair, and the Arabian, which has only one hump and short, sandy-colored or whitish hair; it is a desert beast of burden, surviving great desert heat and tolerating dehydration; found in Africa and Asia

moose   even-toed, hoofed mammal; largest deer in the world; found in the Northern United States and Canada; called "elk" in Europe; it grows to about seven feet and weighs up to 1800 pounds; the male (bull) has two huge, flattened antlers, each shaped like an open hand, and has a bell of fur-covered skin hanging from its neck

Notes on Felines and Other Flesh-Eating Mammals

leopard   flesh-eating (carnivorous); of the cat or feline family; is famous for its *spots*, which are called "rosettes"; no two leopard skins are identical; is the strongest of the flesh eaters; is beautiful, graceful, and dangerous; found in Africa and Asia; its skin is used commercially; one of the fastest animals in the world (the fastest being the *jaguar*)

tiger   flesh-eating; is breathtaking in beauty and power; almost identical in physical structure with the lion; its skin, **claws**, and whiskers are used commercially; found in Asia; someone "tigerish" is brave

lion   flesh-eating; known as the "king of the jungle," a symbol of strength, nobility, and courage, and a person who is "lion-hearted" shares those characteristics; male has a large, yellow *mane*; male is the head of a harem; lions live in groups, called "prides"; found in Africa and Asia

cat   flesh-eating; domesticated relation to the lion, tiger, leopard, panther, and jaguar; is said to have "nine lives"; cats are popular as pets; cats *purr* and *meow*; there are many breeds, such as Siamese, Persian, and Manx

fox   flesh-eating; is a member of the dog family; is sly, quick footed, and yellow eyed; the best-known species is the red fox; foxes live in *dens* and hunt at night; its fur is used commercially

raccoon   flesh-eating; found in North America; is almost as intelligent as the monkey; is a nocturnal animal; eats a lot and is infamous for raiding garbage and campsites; rinses off most of its food before eating; its black mask makes it difficult for enemies to locate the vulnerable pupils of its eyes; its fur is used commercially

skunk   flesh-eating; is a member of the weasel family; when alarmed or attacked, the skunk sprays a sulfide that has an acrid, choking odor and that can temporarily blind an enemy

Notes on Aquatic Mammals

whale   aquatic; there are many different varieties: blue whales, gray whales, humpbacks, devilfish whales, and killer whales or orca (illustrated); the blue whale is the largest mammal that has ever lived on the Earth, including the dinosaurs; below water, whales hold their breath, which, under pressure, is heated and released as a column of vapor through their *spouts*; one of the most intelligent of mammals; is most humanlike in terms of social structure

otter   flesh-eating; its fur is the most beautiful and valuable in the world, but there are severe restrictions on the killing of sea otter

walrus   fin-footed; inhabits the Arctic Ocean; it drifts on ice floes and digs shellfish on the ocean floor; its tusks protect it from the polar bear

seal   fin-footed; there are two types of seals: true, or hair, seals and the eared seals; the harp seal is illustrated; a baby seal is called a calf; true seals have only an opening in their heads instead of external ears; they can stay under water 10 to 20 minutes and dive 200 feet; in aquariums, trained seals perform tricks, such as balancing on one **flipper** and balancing balls on their noses

dolphin   aquatic; belongs to the same order as whales and *porpoises*, and, like them, has a blowhole through which it breathes; communicates with its own kind; has the world's best sonar equipment and keenest auditory sense of any animal

Notes on Primates

monkey   there are many varieties, such as langurs, capuchins, and Rhesus monkeys; known for swinging on trees and eating bananas; "to monkey with" something means "to play with," as in "Don't monkey with that equipment"

gibbon   almost three feet tall; found in Asia and the East Indies; moves through the treetops with the speed of a bird

chimpanzee   the *ape* most like humans; the chimpanzee (chimp) of Africa is the most intelligent of all animals; has memories of visual objects and can use simple tools; adult males are about five feet tall and weigh about 140 pounds

gorilla   fully grown, is more than six feet tall and over 475 pounds; the nails on its fingers and toes are like a human's; is not aggressive towards people; feeds on bamboo shoots, wild celery, and buds from trees; found in Africa

orangutan   a powerful great ape of Borneo and Sumatra; has a large head and arms that reach nearly to the ground; it lives in trees, where it builds nests and feeds on fruit and buds

baboon   a large, terrestrial monkey; lives with its family in a tribe; found in Africa and Asia

Notes on Bears

panda   flesh-eating; is a relative of the raccoon, although early research categorized it as a bear; often referred to as a panda bear; comes from China and the Himalayas; the giant panda (pictured) is playful and a great zoo attraction, but is an endangered species

black bear   flesh-eating; like other bears, it is extremely powerful and capable of great speed; it mates in the summer and *hibernates* in the winter; is found throughout the United States; may be black, chocolate, cinnamon, or light brown in color

polar bear   flesh-eating; inhabits the Arctic Ocean; largest and strongest carnivorous animal on Earth; may weigh up to 1600 pounds and be ten feet tall on its hind legs; divides its time between cold waters and ice floes

grizzly bear   flesh-eating; is large and ferocious; found in western North America; varies in color from grayish to brownish

Notes on Dogs

dog   flesh-eating; domesticated relation to wolves and foxes; known as "man's best friend"

wolf   flesh-eating; is found in Canada, vast areas of Asia, East Europe, Alaska, and several states of the United States; kills cattle, sheep, and smaller animals for food; is called the gray wolf, but is also tawny brown or red; *mates* for its lifetime and lives in a den; scouts for prey in a *pack*

hyena   flesh-eating; found in Africa and Asia; may be striped or spotted; has an eerie howl at night that sounds like wild laughter (hence the expression "laughing hyena"); attacks only easy prey and subsists largely on bones and carrion

Suggested Activities

1. Have the students ask each other questions about the mammals using questions beginning with "Which animal?" such as, "Which animal has a pouch and a powerful tail and stands upright?" or "Which animal from Asia and Africa has spots?"

2. Ask the students to tell a story about any real or imaginary pet that they or someone they know has had.

3. Have students name the mammals indigenous to their native country.

70 & 71   Map of the World

Notes About the Dictionary Page

The Map of the World shown is a geographical map, which indicates significant features of the geography, as opposed to a political map, which shows political boundaries. (See Appendix A for a list, by continent, of the countries of the world and their capital cities.) Mountain ranges are indicated by dark green; deserts are light brown; and rivers are dark blue lines.

Cross-Reference   *Weather (25), Seasonal Verbs (26), Maps (72–73), Appendix A*

Resource Notes

• An atlas (47) is a bound collection of maps. A globe (47) is a spherical depiction of the Earth. There are different kinds of maps, such as *topographical maps*, which show the surface features and elevations of an area; *maritime charts*, which show depths of water and hazards; and *road maps*, which show the roads and indicate what kind of roads they are.

• The Earth is about 29% land and 71% water. **Asia** is the largest of the seven **continents**, with almost 30% of the Earth's land and about 60% of the population. The **Pacific** is the largest **ocean**, and the **South China** is the largest **sea**. The highest mountain is Mount Everest in the **Himalayas** in Asia. The driest place on Earth is the **Atacama Desert** in **South America**, where the rainfall is barely measurable. The longest river in the world is the **Nile** in **Africa**.

• Time zones: The world is divided into 24 longitudinal time zones, each 15° wide, and each representing one hour. Beginning at Greenwich, England, an hour is subtracted, going west, or added, going east, until the *International Date Line* is reached, 12 hours earlier and 12 hours later. The International Date Line is a theoretical line following approximately the 180° meridian, located in the Pacific Ocean.

- Climate: There are five terrestrial *zones* bounded by imaginary lines parallel to the **equator**. The Torrid Zone is bounded by the Tropic of Cancer on the north and the Tropic of Capricorn on the south. The equator runs through the middle of the Torrid Zone, and the climate is *tropical*. The North Temperate Zone is bounded by the Tropic of Cancer and the Arctic Circle. The United States is in the North Temperate Zone, and the climate is *temperate*. The South Temperate Zone is bounded by the Tropic of Capricorn and the Antarctic Circle. The four seasons in the South Temperate Zone are the reverse of the four seasons in the North Temperate Zone. The North Frigid Zone is bounded by the Arctic Circle and the North Pole; the South Frigid Zone is bounded by the Antarctic Circle and the South Pole; the climate is *frigid* in these two zones.

Suggested Activities

1. Have the students pair off and interview each other, asking the following questions: "What city/What country/What continent are you originally from? What are the people from there called? What language do they speak?" Then have each student point to the map and tell the class about the person he/she has just interviewed, as in "Maria is from Lima, Peru, South America. The people there are called Peruvians and they speak Spanish."

2. Have the students "show and tell" about their native countries. They may bring in a traditional article of clothing or a utensil, or they may perform a folk song or folk dance. In any case, they should provide the other students with background information.

3. Have one student ask questions about which continent the mountain ranges, deserts, and rivers are located in. For example, one student asks, "Where is the Sahara Desert?" and another replies, "It's in Africa."

72 & 73 The United States of America

Notes About the Dictionary Page

The states are numbered in alphabetical order to facilitate identification from the map. (See Appendix B for a chart of the states of the United States with their abbreviations, capital cities, and dates of entry into the Union.)

Cross-Reference

Maps (70–71), Appendix B

Culture Notes

- The continental states are grouped *regionally*, but the groupings are not hard and fast. They are usually based on similarities in geography, history, climate, and economy.

New England Connecticut, Maine, Massachusetts, New Hampshire, Rhode Island, Vermont

New England is known for its picturesque villages, autumn scenery, dairy products, and maple syrup. It was originally settled in the 1600s by the Puritans, who first landed at Plymouth Rock. It later became the nation's first industrial center. Its largest city is Boston.

Mid-Atlantic	Delaware, (Maryland,) New Jersey, New York, Pennsylvania, (Virginia)

A major center of international trade, this region is known for its ports and for farming. It is the nation's most densely populated area, containing such prominent cities as New York and Philadelphia.

The South	Alabama, Arkansas, Florida, Georgia, Kentucky, Louisiana, Maryland, Mississippi, North Carolina, South Carolina, Tennessee, (Eastern Texas,) Virginia, West Virginia

Originally, this region's economy was heavily based on agriculture, particularly cotton, but it has boomed as an industrial region since the mid-1900s. Many Southerners have a strong feeling of regional loyalty and take pride in the South's history and traditions (see Civil War below).

The Midwest	Illinois, Indiana, Iowa, Kansas, Michigan, Minnesota, Missouri, Nebraska, North Dakota, Ohio, South Dakota, Wisconsin

A very flat region that is famous for its rich soil and many farms, but that is also home to a number of large cities. The Mississippi River and the Great Lakes are the focal points for industry and transportation.

Rocky Mountain States	Colorado, Idaho, Montana, Nevada, (New Mexico,) Utah, Wyoming

This region is renowned for its scenic beauty, resort areas, and parks. It is the most sparsely populated region of the continental United States, but still has major centers of manufacturing.

The Southwest	Arizona, Southern California, New Mexico, Oklahoma, (Western) Texas

This region is known for its wide open spaces and farms, but its wealth has come from its vast deposits of oil and natural gas. This has made this region the fastest growing in the country in this century.

Pacific Coast States	Northern California, Oregon, Washington

Originally populated during the Gold Rush of the 1800s, this region is now well known for its mild climate and dramatic scenery. It is a center for both manufacturing and farming, and its cities, such as Los Angeles, are among the largest in the country.

- Other regions:

Plains States	Illinois, Iowa, Kansas, Missouri, Nebraska, North Dakota, Oklahoma, South Dakota
Deep South	Alabama, Georgia, Louisiana, Mississippi, South Carolina
Gulf States	Alabama, Florida, Louisiana, Mississippi, Texas
Great Lakes States	Illinois, Indiana, Michigan, Minnesota, New York, Ohio, Wisconsin
Four Corners	Arizona, Colorado, New Mexico, Utah
Pacific Northwest	Northern California, Oregon, Washington
Sun Belt	The states of the South and the Southwest

- States are also grouped together in historical regions. There were 13 *colonies* in America when they rebelled against the rule of Great Britain and formed the United States. They were (in order of statehood): Delaware, Pennsylvania, New Jersey, Georgia, Connecticut, Massachusetts, Maryland, South Carolina, New Hampshire, Virginia, New York, North Carolina, and Rhode Island.

- During the *Civil War*, the United States divided into the *Union* (North) and the *Confederacy* (South). The states of the Union were: Connecticut, Delaware, Illinois, Indiana, Iowa, Kansas, Massachusetts, Michigan, Minnesota, New Hampshire, New Jersey, New York, Ohio, Pennsylvania, Rhode Island, Vermont, and Wisconsin. California and Oregon gave their allegiances to the North but were not directly involved with the conflict.

  The states of the Confederacy were (in order of secession): South Carolina, Mississippi, Florida, Alabama, Georgia, Louisiana, Texas, Virginia, Arkansas, Tennessee, and North Carolina. Border states with divided allegiances were Missouri, Kentucky, West Virginia, and Maryland.

  The dividing line between the North and the South runs along the border of Pennsylvania and Maryland. It is known as the *Mason-Dixon line*.

  The Civil War was fought over the idea of *slavery* and its economic importance to the South. By the mid-1800s, the Northern states had abolished slavery, and the conflict over this issue grew until the Southern states felt they had to *secede* from the United States.

  Although slavery was abolished after the Civil War, inequities between blacks and whites still existed. These were brought to national attention by the Supreme Court rulings regarding desegregation and the *Civil Rights Movement* of the 1950s and 1960s.

Resource Notes

- **Washington, D.C.** (District of Columbia) is not a state, but is the capital of the United States. *Puerto Rico* is a selfgoverning commonwealth whose people are U.S. citizens. *U.S. territories* include the U.S. Virgin Islands, American Samoa, and Guam.

- Major bodies of water—Rivers: Colorado, Ohio, Mississippi, Missouri, Rio Grande; Sounds: Puget Sound, Long Island Sound; Lakes: Great Lakes (Lake Huron, Lake Ontario, Lake Michigan, Lake Erie, Lake Superior), Great Salt Lake

- Major mountain ranges: Sierra Nevadas, Rockies, Blue Mountains, Cascades, Olympic Mountains, Sacramento Mountains, Appalachians, Smokies, White Mountains, Adirondacks, Green Mountains

Suggested Activities

1. Have each student find out one piece of information about a state (which may be the state they live in), such as the state capital, motto, nickname, noun for inhabitants, state parks, visitor attractions, etc. Compile the information for all the students to have as a guide to the state.

2. Some of the students may have lived in a few states or may have traveled around the United States. Ask those students to tell about one state they may have been to, including when they were there, what part of the state they visited, and what their impressions were.

3. Bring in a large physical map of the United States. Have the students identify the major bodies of water and mountain ranges.

74 The Universe

Notes About the Dictionary Page

Section A depicts objects in outer space. The planets are numbered from right to left so that they match the order in which students usually learn their names. Section B depicts the solar and lunar eclipses and the planets of the solar system. Section C depicts phases of the Earth's moon.

Cross-Reference

Space Program (75)

Supplemental Vocabulary

sunrise	sunlight	sunshine	glow
sunset	daylight	(sun's) ray	twinkle
dawn	twilight	(moon's) beam	rise
	dusk		set

Alternate Words

meteor shooting star

Culture Notes

We view the **stars** as magical and mysterious, and we often make wishes on stars. (Star light, star bright,/First star I see tonight,/I wish I may, I wish I might/Have the wish I wish tonight.) A poem by Jane Taylor, "The Star," was extremely popular in the 19th century. The first verse is still well known as a Mother Goose rhyme. (Twinkle, twinkle, little star,/How I wonder what you are!/Up above the world so high/Like a diamond in the sky/Twinkle, twinkle, little star,/How I wonder what you are.)

Notes on A

- The **universe** is everything in creation. Outer space refers to the area beyond the **Earth's** atmosphere. It is occupied by billions of **galaxies** that contain a great variety of objects, such as dust clouds, nebulas, pulsars, and other types of stars. Stars occur in many varieties and are classified by size, temperature, and content. The **Sun** is an average yellow star. Stars may have planets, asteroids, and comets revolving about them in **solar systems**. Planets in turn may have **moons** and **rings** revolving about them. The *Milky Way* is the visible portion of our own galaxy; the name of our galaxy is also the Milky Way.

- The sky is divided into the 12 signs of the *zodiac* (Aquarius, Pisces, Aries, Taurus, Gemini, Cancer, Leo, Virgo, Libra, Scorpio, Sagittarius, and Capricorn), which are named after **constellations**. Constellations are groupings of visible stars that were identified by ancient *astronomers* as points in a picture. In the northern hemisphere, we see the Northern Sky. In the southern hemisphere, we see the Southern Sky. Well-known constellations of the Northern Sky are the Big Dipper, the Little Dipper, and Orion.

- **Comets**, such as Halley's comet, are bodies that **orbit** the Sun, usually in elliptical paths that take them alternately close to and far from the Sun. As they approach the Sun, the pressure of the solar wind causes loose material to spread out from the main body, giving them an elongated shape. **Meteors** are fiery streaks in the sky produced by meteoroids (usually former comets) penetrating the Earth's atmosphere. **Asteroids** are small bodies (from less than a mile to 480 miles in diameter) that orbit the Sun, mostly between the orbits of Mars and Jupiter.

Notes on B

- The Earth is one of nine known **planets** of our solar system. All nine planets occupy their own orbits around the Sun. Mercury is closest to the Sun; next is Venus, then Earth, Mars, Jupiter, Saturn, Uranus, Neptune, and Pluto. All of the planets except for the Earth were named for figures in Roman mythology.

- While the Earth orbits around the Sun, it also rotates on its own *axis*, which is at a certain angle. It takes 24 hours for the Earth to rotate once on its axis. When the part of the Earth we are in rotates away from the Sun, it gets dark, thus creating night.

- It takes approximately 365 days (one *year*) for the Earth to orbit the Sun. The tilt of the Earth's axis causes the length of days and nights to vary during the year as the Earth revolves about the Sun, in turn causing the *seasons* of the year.

Notes on C

- Many of the planets, like Earth, have moons that revolve around them. It takes the **Moon** about 28 days (one month) to revolve around the Earth. The Moon is illuminated by the Sun. Depending on the relative position of the Moon as it revolves around the Earth, we see different portions of the Moon illuminated. The Moon appears to go from invisible (the **new moon**) to a *crescent* (**first quarter**) to a full moon to a crescent again (**last quarter**). The Moon is *waxing* when we perceive it to be increasing in size, and *waning* when we perceive it to be getting smaller. When we look at the full moon, it appears to have a face; we call it "the man in the Moon."

- The gravitational pull of the Moon and the Sun causes the tides. The moon is also said to affect human behavior. The word *lunatic* is derived from the Latin word (luna) for moon.

- A **lunar eclipse** occurs when the Earth passes directly between the Sun and the Moon, blocking the light of the Sun from reaching the Moon. A **solar eclipse** occurs when the Moon passes directly between the Earth and the Sun, obscuring the Sun from view.

Suggested Activities

1. Have one student point to one of the illustrations, and the other students name the object.

2. Teach the students to recite "Twinkle, twinkle, little star" and "Star light, star bright."

3. If feasible, take the students to a local planetarium or observatory.

75 The Space Program

Cross-Reference

Universe (74)

Culture Notes

The U.S. space program is under the jurisdiction of *NASA*, the National Aeronautics and Space Administration, a federal agency. While the **spacecraft** are launched from the Kennedy Space Center in Cape Canaveral, Florida, *mission control* is in Houston, Texas.

Notes on A

Kind of Craft	*Distinguishing Features*
space station	also called *space platform*; a satellite designed to revolve in a fixed orbit; it houses people and serves as a base for scientific observation and experiment, the refueling of spaceships, and the launching of missiles or satellites; *Skylab* was the U.S. space station, which broke up in 1979

communication satellite	receives messages from one place on Earth and transmits them to another place on Earth
weather satellite	has special cameras and instruments for meteorological observation and collection of data
space probe	designed for deep exploration outside the orbit of the Earth within the solar system; equipped with information-gathering instruments, including a large receiving dish

Notes on B

The first **moon landing** took place on July 20, 1969. U.S. Apollo 11 mission **astronauts** Neil Armstrong and Buzz Aldrin successfully touched down on the Moon in their **lunar module** (lunar excursion module, LEM). Neil Armstrong declared, "That's one small step for [a] man, one giant leap for mankind," as he stepped onto the surface of the Moon. There have been a total of six Moon landings by the United States, the only country to have a manned Moon landing.

The **command module** remained in orbit around the Moon with astronaut Mike Collins aboard while the others walked on the Moon. Because the gravitational pull of the Moon is one-sixth that of Earth, the lunar astronauts were much lighter while on the surface (something which weighs 66 pounds on the Earth will only weigh 11 pounds on the Moon).

The command module returned to Earth; it landed in the ocean and was picked up by a waiting aircraft carrier (48).

Notes on C

• The **space shuttle** is distinguished from other spaceships in that it is a reusable spacecraft. It goes into space like a **rocket**, orbits like a **satellite**, and lands like a glider. Its use is primarily commercial, and it carries cargo, or **payloads**. The shuttle was the first spacecraft to carry *civilians* into space.

• On January 28, l986, the space shuttle *Challenger* exploded just after takeoff, killing all seven astronauts aboard. It is considered to be one of this country's greatest tragedies.

Suggested Activities

1. Have one student point to one of the illustrations, and the other students name the object.

2. Have the students go to the library and research the astronauts who flew on one of the original space flights, the Apollo mission, or a shuttle flight. Have each student write a paragraph about one of the astronauts and share it with the class.

76 A Classroom

Cross-Reference

School Verbs (77)

Supplemental Vocabulary

pledge allegiance	do homework	learn	sign
teach	take notes	study	measure
instruct	copy the assignment	sharpen	circle
hang up	glue	erase	put up
put away	paste	change	take down
type	brush on	write	stand up
key in	apply	print	sit down

Alternate Words	**chalkboard**	blackboard
	thumbtack	tack
	student	pupil

Usage Notes

There are certain guidelines that determine how **students** should address **teachers** in this country. In elementary through high school, teachers are normally addressed as Mr., Ms., Miss, Mrs., or Dr. In *postsecondary programs*, teachers may be addressed formally as above (with the addition of Professor) or informally by their first names.

Culture Notes

Education is very important in the United States. Many jobs require at least a *high school diploma* from employees, and most "white-collar" jobs require a *college degree*. It is desirable to obtain at least the high school diploma, and older people who do not have one can get a General Educational Development diploma by studying for and taking the *General Educational Development Test* (GED). This is also known as a high school equivalency exam.

Resource Notes

- School systems: Each municipality has its own school system, and variations exist depending on the size of the *school district*. School is compulsory for children beginning at about age six (first grade) until age 16.

- Most school systems have the following divisions:

  nursery school

elementary/grade school	kindergarten through fifth grade or kindergarten through sixth grade
intermediate/middle school	sixth through eighth grade or seventh through ninth grade (*junior high school*)
high school	ninth through twelfth grade; freshman, sophomore, junior, and senior years

- Some private or parochial schools may be set up differently, with elementary school going from kindergarten through eighth grades. Certain private schools are called *prep schools* and specifically prepare students for college.

- After high school, people may go to postsecondary programs, which include two-year *colleges* (community colleges), four-year colleges, adult schools, job training programs, etc.

Suggested Activities

1. Write the words listed on this page and any additional words (nouns) you have given on separate index card. Have each student pick a card and tape it to the appropriate object in your classroom.

2. Have each student write a sentence for one of the words listed. Help the students to be sure their sentences are correct. Collect the sentences, put them all on a worksheet, leaving out the vocabulary word listed, thus creating a fill-in-the-blank worksheet for the students.

3. Have the students tell a story about the class in the picture, using the vocabulary listed and any additional words you have given.

77 School Verbs

Notes About the Dictionary Page	The verbs illustrated on this page are presented in the context of school, but may be used in a variety of contexts in our speech.
Cross-Reference	*Classroom (76)*
Language Notes	**read**/read/read **write**/wrote/written **tear**/tore/torn **draw**/drew/drawn **leave**/left/left

Supplemental Vocabulary

participate	read out loud	turn in (an assignment)	pass
ask questions	take a test	be in the (X) grade	fail
answer questions	hand out	graduate (from)	register
call on	take out	get an (alphabetical	enroll
recite	put away	or numerical) grade	pay tuition
get up	go to school	get promoted	

Resource Notes

Verb	Typical Objects	Related Verbs
raise	one's hand (4), one's voice	put up, yell
touch	your nose (4), a button (101)	press
erase	the chalkboard (76), a mistake	wipe clean, correct
read	a book, a map	study
close	a door, a notebook (76)	shut
listen (to)	a story, a lecture, music	pay attention
write	a composition, a report	draft, revise
walk (to)	school, home, come, go	
tear	a piece of paper, a page	rip
type	an essay, a term paper	proofread
draw	a picture, a diagram	sketch, paint
tie	a shoe(lace) (20), a bow	fasten
leave	the room, the class	go out
enter	the building, the (n)th grade	come in

Suggested Activities

1. Give the students the first two headings of the columns above. Provide them with the verb in the first column, and ask them to list as many words as they can to go along with each verb. Provide examples to get them started, if appropriate.

2. Have the students write a paragraph about their daily school routine, using the vocabulary listed and any additional words you have given.

3. Have the students make up a sentence about each illustration that describes the action and a motive. For example, "The girl is raising her hand to ask a question," "The girl is touching her nose in the game," etc.

78 A Science Lab

Notes About the Dictionary Page	This is a typical school science lab. The items pictured are used in different branches of science.
Cross-Reference	*Classroom (76), School Verbs (77), Math (79), Appendix C*
Resource Notes	*Science* is a general term that includes *biology, chemistry, physics*, and *earth science*. **Lab** (laboratory) work gives students an opportunity to practice the scientific method; that is, to perform *experiments* in order to test *hypotheses* through observations.

Apparatus Used in All Areas of Chemistry

flask	container; comes in varying shapes and sizes; lets a *scientist* observe a *reaction*; those shown are Erlenmeyer flasks (the narrow necks reduce *evaporation*)
beaker	container; used when a scientist wants to be able to reach inside the container easily
graduated cylinder	a container that has delineations to show the *volume* of a liquid
pipette	used to transfer liquids; a narrow tube, tapered at one end, that is usually graduated to show the volume of what is being transferred
medicine dropper	a type of pipette, but is not graduated; approximate measurement is done by counting the number of drops released
scale	a counter scale; the object to be weighed is put on one side of the scale and **weights** are put on the other side until the two sides *balance*; the weights are totaled to determine the object's weight
Bunsen burner	a cylindrically shaped burner in which flammable gas and air are mixed and ignited with a match to produce an intensely hot, almost invisible flame
ring stand	a stand with an adjustable ring for supporting containers

Apparatus Used in Biology Courses

petri dish	a shallow glass dish with a loose-fitting cover, usually filled with agar or another culture medium and in which bacterial *cultures* are grown
microscope	used for visually enlarging very small objects so they can be examined; the object is placed on a **slide**, which fits under the lens of the microscope
dissection kit	a set of instruments used to dissect animals

Apparatus Used in Physics Courses

prism	refracts light into the colors of the *spectrum*
magnet	attracts iron and produces a *magnetic field* (a horseshoe magnet, a bar magnet, north/positive pole, south/negative pole, attract, repel)

Suggested Activities	1. Have one student point to a picture and the other students name the object. If possible, have the students go to the science lab and point to the actual object.
	2. Present the students with various situations they would encounter as scientists, and ask them to identify what apparatus they would need in each case. For example, "What apparatus do you need if you are a biologist who needs to examine a drop of water," etc.

79 Math

Cross-Reference	*Classroom (76), School Verbs (77), Science (78), Appendix* C
Alternate Words	oval ellipse
Usage Notes	**Math** is the short form of *mathematics,* which we use as a singular noun, as in "Mathematics is my favorite subject." Math is a general term that includes arithmetic, algebra, (plane) geometry, trigonometry, solid geometry, calculus, etc.
Resource Notes	The four basic arithmetic functions are *addition, subtraction, multiplication,* and *division.* The four arithmetic functions are performed on all numbers—whole numbers, fractions, decimals, percentages, exponents, signed numbers (negative and positive), etc.
Notes on A	Laws in geometry related to lines: The shortest path between two points is a **straight line. Parallel lines** never meet. **Perpendicular lines** always meet at a 90° angle.

Notes on B

Shape	*Distinguishing Features*
right angle	90°
obtuse angle	between 91° and 180°
acute angle	between 0° and 89°
triangle	all triangles have three sides and the total of the three angles is always 180°; an *isosceles triangle* has two equal sides; an *equilateral triangle* has three equal sides; in a **right triangle**, one of the angles of the triangle is a right angle ($a^2 + b^2 = c^2$, where c is the **hypotenuse** of a right triangle); a straight line drawn from the **base** of a triangle to its **apex** is the *altitude* of the triangle; the *formula* for the area of a triangle is one-half of the base times the altitude
circle	all circles are closed curves, every point of which is equidistant from the **center**; the **radius** is any straight line from the center of the circle to its **circumference**; the **diameter** is any straight line that bisects the circle (divides it in half); the formula for the circumference of a circle is πd or $2\pi r$; the formula for the area of a circle is πr^2; an **arc** is a segment of the circumference; a **section** is the area within two radii
parallelogram	all parallelograms have four sides with opposite sides parallel; the total of the four angles is always 360°; a **rectangle** is a parallelogram that has four right angles; a **square** is a parallelogram that has four equal sides and four right angles; the formula for the area of a parallelogram is the length times the width

Notes on C	Solid figures are *three-dimensional.* A **cube** is a three-dimensional square; a *sphere* is a three-dimensional circle; a **pyramid** is a three-dimensional triangle.
Notes on D	numerator the top number in a **fraction**
	denominator the bottom number in a fraction

lowest common denominator	the lowest number that two fractions can both have as denominators; for example, twelfths is the lowest common denominator of a quarter and a third
proper fraction	a fraction whose numerator is less than its denominator
improper fraction	a fraction whose numerator is greater than its denominator

Notes on E   See Appendix *C* for a table of metric conversions.

units of measure:	fraction of an inch, inch, fraction of a foot, foot, yard
dimensions:	a x b x c (**width** x **height** x **depth**)
tools:	ruler (76), tape measure (36, 101), yardstick

Suggested Activities

1. If appropriate, review the numbers from one to 1,000,000.

2. Have the students create one of their own addition, subtraction, multiplication, and division examples with whole numbers. Have them solve the problems and then tell the class the steps they took.

3. If appropriate, demonstrate how to read a ruler. Have the students measure objects in the room (a desk top, a shelf, a bulletin board, etc.) and report to the other what the dimensions of the object are.

80 Energy

Notes About the Dictionary Page

This page is divided up into A: the resources used for producing energy; B: the means by which these resources are turned into energy; and C: the end result, either in type of energy or in product.

Culture Notes

Energy *conservation* became popular in the United States after the oil shortages of the mid-1970s. Today most energy companies offer information to customers on how to conserve energy in their homes, cars, and offices.

Notes on A and B

- **Oil, natural gas,** and **coal** are considered natural resources and are termed "fuel" for various types of power. Oil is found underground by drilling, which could be on land or offshore. Because of its value, it is nicknamed "black gold." Before it is refined it is called crude oil.

- Another resource not mentioned is *uranium*, from which is generated nuclear (atomic) energy.

- Energy from the **Sun** is called *solar energy*.

- Energy from water that is turned into electrical energy, either by harnessing the force as from a **waterfall** or from blocking it by a **dam**, is called *hydroelectric* power. Another way to generate energy from water is to heat it, creating *steam*.

- Energy from **geysers** is called *geothermal* power.

• Electrical power is obtained by converting one form of energy (mechanical, water, steam, etc.) into electrical energy, as when fuel is burned, which converts water to steam that drives *turbines* that turn **generators** in a **power station**; the **electricity** is sent by **transmission towers** through **power lines** to **utility poles**. **Transformers** mounted on utility poles convert the *voltage* and *current* so that it can be used by consumers.

Notes on C

• There are many other uses and products not listed here.

• Heat can be of different types, such as steam (pictured), which is most likely produced by a burner fueled by oil, natural gas, or coal.

• Electricity, as has been noted, can be produced from various sources.

• **Gasoline** is different from natural gas, and is used mostly for automobiles. In the United States there are a few types of gas: leaded, unleaded, regular, and premium. For environmental reasons, leaded gas is used much less, mostly for older cars.

• **Motor oil** is used for most kinds of engines, including car engines, and boat motors.

• **Diesel fuel** is used for trucks, diesel-fueled cars, and trains.

Suggested Activities

1. Bring in pictures from magazines that illustrate the types of energy listed above. For example, you can bring in pictures of a fireplace, an electric appliance, a sailboat, and a steam locomotive. Have the students ask each other questions beginning with "Which type of energy provides power?" such as, "Which type of energy provides power to the sailboat?"

2. Have the students go to the library and do research on one of the types of energy illustrated. Have each student give an oral report to the other students.

3. For each of the illustrations in Picture C, have the students write a sentence using the vocabulary listed and any additional words you have given.

81 Farming and Ranching

Notes About the Dictionary Page

Picture A shows a dairy farm that also has orchards. The dairy cows and and sheep are grazing in the pasture. The farmer is feeding the chickens in the barnyard. Picture B shows a wheat farm. The farmer is using the combine to harvest the wheat. A scarecrow is in the field to keep the birds from destroying the crop. Livestock—cows, pigs, and roosters—are in the barnyard. Picture C shows a cattle ranch. The cowhands are herding the cattle, which are raised for beef. There are horses in the corral. (There are many other kinds of farms and ranches, some of which are noted below.)

Cross-Reference

Animals (64, 66–67), Maps (72–73)

Supplemental Vocabulary

• plant	raise	harvest	produce
grow	till	cultivate	graze

- The vocabulary listed can be grouped according to the following categories.

buildings	farmhouse, silo, barn
land	farmland, pasture, field
enclosed areas	barnyard, corral, chicken coop, pigpen
personnel	farmer, rancher, farmhand, ranchhand, cowboy, cowgirl
tools	pitchfork, brand, poke
machines	tractor, combine, plow
livestock	sheep (67), dairy cows (67), cattle, horses (67), chickens (64), pigs, goats (67)

Language Notes

combine   [kŏm′ bīn]

Culture Notes

- Farming was the way the United States was originally tamed and settled. Today the image of a *family farm* in the *heartland* of America remains a popular symbol of the United States to most Americans.

- The song "Old MacDonald Had a Farm" is sung by little children learning the names of the farm animals and the sounds associated with them.

Resource Notes

- A **farmhouse** is a farmer's residence. A **silo** is used for storing *fodder*, feed for **livestock**. A **barn** is used for storing grain/hay and housing **cattle** and **horses**; the haymow is the top level of the barn, where hay is stored.

- A **tractor** is used for pulling farm machinery. A **combine** is a harvesting machine. A *plow* is used to till the land in preparation for planting.

General Category	*Specific Type*
farm	animals: dairy, poultry, pig
	crops: wheat, soybean, potato
orchard	apple, cherry, peach
grove	citrus (orange, lemon, etc.), pecan, olive
plantation	sugar, cotton, coffee
vineyard	grapes
ranch	cattle, horses, sheep

Kind of Farm/Ranch	*States Where Primarily Found*
wheat	Indiana, Illinois, Iowa, Kansas, Nebraska, South Dakota
corn	Indiana, Illinois, Iowa, Kansas, Nebraska
dairy	New England States, New York, Pennsylvania, Minnesota, Wisconsin, Virginia, California
cattle	Texas, Oklahoma, Colorado, Wyoming
vineyard	California, New York

Suggested Activities

1. Have the students tell a story about the people in each of the illustrations, using the vocabulary listed and any additional words you have given them.

2. Bring in a recording of "Old MacDonald." Have the students point to the picture of each animal as it is introduced in the song.

3. Bring in a news story about farmers in this country. If necessary, rewrite the story in simplified terms. Explain the background information and issues before giving the article to the students to read.

82 Construction

Notes About the
Dictionary Page

Construction work may involve the building trades, as in Picture A, or road repair and maintenance, as in Picture B.

Cross-Reference *Clothes (19–21), Workshop (36–37), Trucks (49), Occupations (84–86)*

Usage Notes People who wear **hard hats** on the job are referred to as hard hats also.

Culture Notes **Construction workers** are also called "blue-collar workers" because of the color of their work clothes and as opposed to "white-collar workers," who wear suits and have desk jobs.

Notes on A

• Construction sites are designated as "hard hat areas"; only people wearing hard hats are permitted near the area for reasons of safety. Construction crews may be involved in *demolition* and *clearing* work as well as construction work.

• The owner of the property (an individual or a *developer*) retains an architect (86) to design a structure, which may be residential, industrial, or commercial. The result of the architect's work is the **blueprints**. A building *contractor* is hired to do the work. The **builder** hires the construction crew, which includes masons, bricklayers, roofers, carpenters (84), plumbers (84), electricians (84), and painters (84).

• In addition to new construction, workers may do remodeling, renovations, restorations, additions, expansions, modernizing, and alterations.

Notes on B

Road crews may be involved in emergency repair and maintenance as well as construction work. They are employed by the government and may work any of three *shifts*: first (day) shift, second shift, and third (night) shift.

Heavy Equipment	Distinguishing Features
cherry picker	a small crane with a semi-enclosed platform at the end of a boom that allows a worker to reach a high place
jackhammer	a handheld power drill, usually connected to a portable generator; used for drilling rock, concrete
backhoe	a truck with a scooplike digging device used for excavations
bulldozer	a tractor-driven pushing blade for clearing land
crane (58)	a device used for lifting and moving heavy materials

Suggested Activities

1. Have the students tell a story about the crews in each of the pictures, using the vocabulary listed and any additional words you have given them.

2. Have the students go to nearby construction sites and interview the construction workers during their lunch or coffee breaks. The student can ask general questions about the work the worker does, or about the specific site he/she is on. Then each student must report back to the class.

83 An Office

Notes About the Dictionary Page

The office depicted is a small business office, with most of the workers working in cubicles.

Cross-Reference

Clothes (20–21), Occupations (84, 86)

Language Notes

Word processor can mean both a computer used for word processing and the person who does the word processing.

Resource Notes

- *Office (clerical) workers* include switchboard operators, typists, word processors, secretaries, stenographers, office managers, bookkeepers, file clerks, mailroom clerks, etc. Most work from 9:00 A.M. to 5:00 P.M., get an hour for lunch, and get two coffee breaks.

Job Title	*Sample of Duties*
switchboard operator	works the switchboard; routes calls, takes messages
typist/word processor	enters information; edits text on screen; prints out hard copies (**printouts**)
secretary	screens calls; places calls; gives messages; returns calls; makes appointments; keeps a **calendar**; schedules meetings; types letters; opens mail
file clerk	files away all incoming and outgoing *correspondence* and related documents; pulls files when they are requested; maintains files in (usually alphabetical, numerical, or chronological) order
office manager	oversees office operations; coordinates projects; distributes work; in charge of *personnel*; has responsibility for office supplies and equipment
stenographer	takes *dictation*; transcribes notes; types transcript
bookkeeper	enters, tallies, and balances all financial records in *ledger books* or on computer *spreadsheets*
mailroom clerk	sorts mail; distributes or delivers mail; takes care of outgoing mail

- *Office equipment* includes word processors, typewriters, computers, calculators, and photocopiers (desktop or console).

- *Office supplies* include file folders, message pads, legal or letter-size white or yellow pads, paper clips, staplers, staples, staple removers, and business stationery (letterhead paper and envelopes).

Suggested Activities

1. Bring the students into the office at school. Have them identify the office equipment and supplies they see. (If this is not possible, have one student point to the picture, and the other students name the object.)

2. Have the students tell a story about each of the workers in the picture, using the vocabulary listed and any additional words you have given them.

3. Have the students interview a clerical worker in an office. What is the person's job title? What does the person do? What does the person like best about the job? Have the students report back to the class.

84 Occupations I: Main Street USA

<table>
<tr>
<td>Notes About the
Dictionary Page</td>
<td>This scene shows the exteriors of businesses on a typical Main Street in the United States. Most of the professions shown on this page have existed for hundreds of years. The cutaways on the roofs let us have a look inside and see the people who work there. The perspective allows us to see only one side of the streets; usually there are businesses on both sides.</td>
</tr>
</table>

Cross-Reference

Office (83), Occupations (85–86). Numerous occupations appear throughout the Dictionary *(15, 16, 39, 42, 43, 46, 47, 48, 49, 53, 54–55, 56, 57, 75, 76, 81, 82, 88, 90, 92, 94, 99).*

Supplemental Vocabulary

shopkeepers/storeowners/merchants/proprietors

Alternate Words

pharmacist	druggist
tailor (m.)	seamstress (f.)
hairdresser	hair stylist

Usage Notes

• When we go to Main Street, we say we are going "to do some shopping" ("pick up a few things, " "run some errands").

• We often refer to the place we're going as "the tailor's, baker's, hairdresser's," etc.

Culture Notes

Small towns and city neighborhoods still have main streets where people can go to do all their shopping, but in many places, "Main Street" is a *shopping center*, a *mall*, or a giant supermarket (14).

Person	*Activities*	*Place*
pharmacist	fills prescriptions; dispenses pharmaceuticals; is called "Dr."	pharmacy/drugstore (45)
mechanic	repairs engines (51); fixes *flat tires*; does *tune-ups*; services car	service station/gas station
barber	cuts (men's) hair; gives shaves	barber shop
travel agent	arranges trips; makes (hotel) *reservations*; issues airline tickets; plans *itineraries*	travel agency
repair person	repairs and reconditions radios, TVs (100), and appliances	repair shop
tailor	alters (takes in, lets out, shortens hems [101]) and mends clothes	tailor's shop/dry cleaners
greengrocer	sells fruits (8–9), vegetables (6–7), dairy products, etc.	fruit and vegetable market/store (45)
baker	bakes bread, cookies, pies, candy; decorates cakes	bake shop/bakery (44)
optician	makes and fits eyeglasses according to the prescription of the *optometrist* or *ophthalmologist* (M.D.)	eye doctor's/eyeglass store/optician's

hairdresser	cuts, styles, colors (dyes, bleaches frosts), straightens, perms, curls, sets, blows out hair	hairdresser's/beauty salon
florist	makes flower (60) arrangements, centerpieces, presentation bouquets, corsages	florist's
jeweller	*appraises* jewelry (23); sets stones; repairs watches; sizes rings	jewelry store
butcher	cuts and prepares meat; dresses poultry (10–11)	butcher's/butcher's shop/ meat market

Suggested Activities

1. For each of the people in the illustrations, have the students write a sentence about the person and something he/she did as part of his/her job on a given day. For example, "Dr. Jones filled Mrs. Martinez's prescription on Monday."

2. There are many more stores not illustrated in the picture. Have the students add as many stores as possible to the 13 illustrated, giving the word for the proprietor (or person who works there). For example, "Like-Nu Dry Cleaning—drycleaner."

85 Occupations II

Notes About the Dictionary Page

This page consists of more occupations, mostly "blue-collar."

Cross-Reference

Housework Verbs (38), Occupations (84, 86)

Alternate Words

housekeeper	cleaning lady/maid

Usage Notes

In conversation, we may ask, "What do you do (for a living)?" or "What kind of work do you do?" The reply may be any of the following basic responses: "I'm a(n) _____," "I work for (kind of company)," "I own my own _____ business," or "I'm unemployed/retired."

Resource Notes

The occupation determines the way a person is paid. For example, a **plumber** may charge a flat amount for the job done; a **real estate agent** will be paid on *commission*; a **housekeeper** will be paid an *hourly salary*; a **factory worker** will be paid an hourly salary plus *overtime*; a **delivery boy** will earn an hourly salary plus *tips*; a shopkeeper will draw a *salary* from the business; a bank officer will be paid an annual salary.

Some occupations are unionized and *wages* are set by the *union*. *Minimum wage* is the amount determined by Congress to be the lowest hourly salary permissible. If you are paid "off the books," there is no official record of your receiving payment.

Notes on A

• There are many services required for maintaining or building a house. Often a *contractor* will be the person hired to subcontract work to various people, such as plumbers, **electricians**, etc.

• Plumbers, electricians, and real estate agents must be *state-licensed*.

Notes on B
- Hotels, hospitals, and other large facilities have their own housekeeping departments. Cleaning services provide *janitors* and housekeepers to commercial buildings, and private agencies provide bonded housekeepers, usually on a per diem basis, to private homeowners.

- Young people often need to get part-time jobs after school and on weekends in order to make pocket money. Males tend to get jobs as delivery boys and females tend to get jobs as *babysitters*. (Both males and females also get jobs in retail stores, fast food restaurants, etc.) Most of these jobs pay the minimum wage. Many older, retired people take these jobs when they are not filled by younger workers.

Notes on C
Most factories are run as *assembly lines*; **shop workers** are also called assembly line workers. Many factories operate 24 hours, with three *shifts* of work: first shift (7 A.M. to 4 P.M.), second shift (4 P.M. to 12 A.M.), and third shift (12 A.M. to 7 A.M.).

Suggested Activities
1. Have the students tell a story about each of the people numbered in the pictures, using the vocabulary listed and any additional words you have given them.

2. There are numerous other occupations on other pages of the Dictionary. Have the students review the pages mentioned above and list all the occupations from those pages. Pair the students and have them ask each other what they do for a living, where they work, and what their hours are. The students can choose to answer with the truth or with something made up from their list.

86 Occupations III

Notes About the Dictionary Page
This page consists of "white-collar" jobs. Section A shows occupations that are not typical office jobs, but are done in studios or at home as freelance employees.

Cross-Reference
Occupations (84–85)

Usage Notes
The word *job* is sometimes used as a synonym for work, as in "He likes his new job," or to mean part of one's occupation, as in "It's the secretary's job to answer the phones." A *career* is an occupation for which one trains and that is undertaken as a permanent calling, as in "She has had a distinguished career as an anthropologist." The word *profession* applies to an occupation involving long and intensive study, scholarly pursuits, and a commitment to public service, as in "They have made great contributions to the medical profession." Career and profession are often used interchangeably.

Culture Notes
- *Job hunting* involves the skills related to reading the *want ads* (classified section); filling out job applications or writing *resumés*; calling for appointments or writing *cover letters*; interviewing; following up on the interview; and negotiating.

- Most Americans start working at *part-time jobs* when they are teenagers. They begin full-time employment after they complete high school (age 18) or college (age 22). Most people work until age 65, though there are companies that allow employees to work until they are 70 or let them take early retirement before 65.

- Most full-time employees receive two weeks of *vacation* and a number of *sick days* each year. The exact amount of either depends on the company. In other companies, both vacation and sick days can increase with the amount of time one is employed. *National holidays* are officially designated by the government, and many companies give these as days off also.

	General	*Specific Examples*
Notes on A	TV reporter	newscaster, anchorperson, weather forecaster (meteorologist), sportscaster, reviewer
	artist	painter, sculptor, illustrator, graphic artist
	photographer	fashion photographer, studio photographer, landscape photographer
	model	fashion model, artist's model
	fashion designer	clothing designer, furniture designer, interior decorator
	writer	novelist, poet, journalist, technical writer, copywriter

Notes on B

The bank **officer** helps customers with specialized bank services and products. The **teller** handles normal banking transactions, deposits, withdrawals, check-cashing, and payrolls.

Notes on C

The computer field has created many new jobs in the last two decades or so. *Systems analysts* determine the hardware and software requirements of a computer installation and maintain the computer's operating systems. **Computer programmers** write computer programs in computer languages compatible with a particular machine so that the computers (100) can be used by others (users) to retrieve information, get reports, etc. *Data entry operators* are the people who put the information into a form the computer can read and process. *Computer operators* are the people who work on large mainframe computers, loading in the information produced by the data entry operators, running the programs, and handling the printouts.

Suggested Activities

1. Have the students tell a story about each of the people in the pictures, using the vocabulary listed and any additional words you have given them.

2. Bring in the classified section of the local Sunday newspapers. Teach the students how to read the want ads, and have them circle any job they may be interested in (in reality or fantasy). Pair the students and have them roleplay the applicant calling the company to inquire about the job in the ad.

87 Neighborhood Parks

Notes About the Dictionary Page
The scene depicts a good-sized park, most likely in a city or large town. Most town parks are smaller and contain recreational equipment only.

Cross-Reference
Outdoor Activities (88–89), Ballfields (93), Sports Verbs (96–97)

Alternate Words

jungle gym	monkey bars
seesaw	teeter-totter
merry-go-round	carousel

Culture Notes
Neighborhood parks, particularly when the weather is warm and fair, are crowded with people of all ages. Parents take little children to the park to go to the **playground**, rides, and **zoo**. Older children play ball, ride bikes, and go swimming. Teenagers "hang out." Adults go jogging, horseback riding, or hiking. Senior citizens play checkers, read books, and attend concerts. People of all ages play on the sports grounds, tennis courts, and basketball courts.

Resource Notes

- Parks are under local (city or town), county, state, or national jurisdiction.

- In part, the size of the park will determine what facilities are available.

Item	Distinguishing Features
zoo	may be a *petting zoo* or *children's zoo*, or have a number of different houses (the reptile house, the monkey house, etc.); zoos may also be separate parks and may have natural habitats for the animals
band shell	also called an amphitheater; for concerts, theater, and other performances
jogging paths	marked with mile markers for joggers/runners
playground	usually has swings (including kiddie swings for toddlers), a **slide**, a **jungle gym**, a **seesaw**, and a **sandbox**
children's rides	**merry-go-rounds**, trains, ferris wheels
horseback riding	horses and ponies for children are available for riding
swimming	may be a lake, a pool, a wading pool, and/or a **sprinkler**
bike paths	paved paths for biking away from pedestrians
ballfields (93)	for softball, volleyball (92), touch football, etc.
hiking trails	blazed (marked) trails in the woods
marina	for motorboats and sailboats (59) to dock
picnic grounds (88)	for *barbecues*

Suggested Activities

1. Have the students describe the scene illustrated, using the vocabulary listed and any additional words you have given them.

2. Have the students tell about a real or imaginary time they went to the park, including the name and location of the park they went to, who they went with, and what they did.

88 & 89 Outdoor Activities

Notes About the Dictionary Page

This scene depicts a not-so-real state or national park, where the major activities have been condensed and merged so that they appear to be happening next to each other.

Cross-Reference

Clothes (19), Beach (90–91), Sports (94–95)

Usage Notes

We use the expression *go + gerund*, as in the following examples: go hiking, go fishing, go picnicking, go rafting, go camping, go backpacking, go mountain climbing, etc.

Culture Notes

• People who like *the great outdoors* spend weekends, holidays, and vacations doing such activities as camping, fishing, and hiking. They go to state and national parks, which, while providing opportunities for recreation, also preserve the natural *wilderness*.

• There are many *clubs* that children and teenagers can join that involve outdoor activities and sports, such as the Boy Scouts, Girl Scouts, 4-H Clubs, and Campfire Girls. While these are national organizations, each *troop* plans its own activities.

Resource Notes

For **hiking,** you generally need *hiking boots*, which provide traction and give ankle support. **Hikers** sometimes carry a *walking stick*, which is often just a fallen tree branch, to help them in climbing or to test the ground they are about to step onto. Although blazed trails may be well marked, hikers should carry *compasses* to keep themselves from getting lost. Hiking *gear*, like *maps*, water bottles, and *first-aid kits*, can be carried in backpacks (19) or fanny packs. Some hikers prefer to bushwhack, or hike off-trail.

Notes on Fishing

Fishing (angling) can be done from boats, from the shore, or standing in the water. Different techniques and equipment are appropriate for each, and the kinds of fish you catch vary with the depth of the water and whether the water is *fresh* or *saltwater*. In general, *fishing tackle* includes a **rod**, *reel, hook*, **line**, and *sinker*. To attract fish, you use either *bait*, which is live, or a *lure*, which is artificial.

Usage Notes

We use the expression "hook, line, and sinker" to mean "the whole thing," as in "They believed the story—hook, line, and sinker." We tell people to "fish or cut bait" when we want them to choose a definite course of action, particularly when they have been procrastinating.

Notes on Picnic Area

Picnic areas have **picnic tables** and **grills** (barbecue pits). People can eat packed sandwiches or have *barbecues* (cookouts). Many people have large picnics with clubs or groups, or annual family reunions. Typical picnic fare includes hamburgers (18), hot dogs (18), spare ribs, and chicken for barbecuing; baked beans (18), salads (18), and watermelon (9).

Notes on Rafting

Rafting is one kind of boating done on rivers or streams. People also take out canoes and kayaks (59). If the water has **rapids**, it is called *white water*. Navigating on white water requires special skills, especially avoiding rocks under the water. Boaters wear life jackets (59) (life vests) as a safety precaution in case the boat *capsizes*.

Notes on Mountain Climbing	**Mountain climbing** that does not involve equipment is called free climbing; climbing that involves equipment is called technical climbing. The equipment includes **harnesses, ropes**, and *pitons* (spikes you put into the cliff).

Notes on Camping

- There are all degrees of "roughing it." People can camp out in the wild, reserve a spot at a *campsite* that has showers and lavatories, or spend their nights in their campers (53) or recreational vehicles (*RVs*).

  Campground fees vary from park to park and are different for individual campsites and group campsites. Individual campsites are available on a first come, first served basis. Reservations are usually required for group campsites.

  Campers *make camp* (set up camp), which includes pitching a tent and building a **campfire**. It is customary for a group of people camping together to roast marshmallows and tell stories or sing songs around the campfire. Campers cook on portable **camp stoves**, which generally use propane fuel (80). When the campers leave their campsite for good, they *break camp*.

- Children often go to *summer camp* (sleep-away camp), where they participate in such outdoor activities as swimming, boating, and hiking. Depending on the camp's focus, they may learn outdoor *survival skills*, including such skills as how to build a fire, how to identify edible plants and berries, and how to avoid poisonous plants (61). There are also adult camps, whose offerings range from social activities to extreme physical challenges.

Suggested Activities

1. Have the students describe the scene in as much detail as they can. For example, "A family is hiking up a trail. The mother is carrying a walking stick and a trail map, and the father is wearing a backpack. Their son is walking behind them."

2. Have the students talk about any (real or imaginary) experiences they have had camping, fishing, hiking, or doing any other outdoor activity. Students should include details about the place they went to, who they were with, what kind of day (weather) it was, what they did, etc.

90 & 91 At the Beach

Notes About the Dictionary Page

This scene depicts, most likely, an East Coast beach, since there is a boardwalk, sand dunes, and a motel close to the beach.

Cross-Reference

Boating (59), Sports Verbs (96–97)

Alternate Words

sunglasses	shades (colloq.)
bathing suit	swimsuits/suits
bathing trunks	swimming trunks

Culture Notes

There are **beaches** on the different bodies of water in the United States: on the Pacific Ocean, the Atlantic Ocean, the Gulf of Mexico, the Intracoastal Waterway on the East Coast, the Great Lakes, and sounds and lakes throughout the country. The **sand** varies in color and texture from region to region; the water varies in color, temperature, calmness, and depth. Some beaches are *public* and others are *private* or open only to residents of a certain area.

Resource Notes

- Beaches are open all year, but where there are four seasons, **lifeguards** are on duty only during the *summer season*, which goes from Memorial Day weekend to Labor Day weekend. Lifeguards are strong swimmers, trained and certified in American Red Cross life-saving procedures. When lifeguards are not on duty, swimming is "at your own risk."

- Some East Coast beaches have **boardwalks**, one of the most famous of which is in Atlantic City, NJ. (The Miss America Beauty Pageant takes place there, and the game Monopoly uses the Boardwalk and Atlantic City street names on its board.) Along the boardwalk, there may be hotels, **refreshment stands**, and souvenir shops.

- **Sand dunes** are sand hills or ridges formed by the wind. The plants that live among the dunes keep them intact by mollifying the effect of the wind and by keeping the sand attached to their roots. People are prohibited from climbing on the dunes to protect the delicate plant life.

- *Beachwear* is the general term applied to clothing worn at the beach or pool. Men and women wear **bathing suits**. Women may wear one-piece bathing suits, two-piece suits, or bikinis; coverups are fashionable, often coordinated, outfits to wear over suits. Men may wear **bathing trunks** or bikinis. **Sunglasses** are worn as both eye protection from the glare of the sun as well as fashion items. To protect the eyes in the water, people wear *goggles*.

- Since *suntans* are associated with attractiveness and good health, many people go to the beach to sunbathe. However, the sun's ultraviolet rays can damage the skin, causing premature wrinkles and skin cancer, so people are cautioned to reduce their exposure to the sun. **Sunbathers** are advised to use **suntan lotion** or suntan oil that contains *sun block*. Sun blocks come in a range of strengths; the higher the SPF (sun protection factor), the more protection. People at the beach lie on **beach towels**, *beach blankets*, **beach chairs**, or lounge chairs (27).

- Beach activities: Little children like to play with **pails** and **shovels** in the sand. As they get older, they may start building **sandcastles**. Adults may build elaborate and quite beautiful sandcastles. Kids and adults alike will collect **shells**, toss **beach balls**, play **Frisbee**, fly **kites**, and play paddleball. Adults may also go running and play volleyball (94).

- Water activities: Near the shore, people float on **air mattresses**, sit in inflatable **tubes**, go *kickboarding*, and swim.

  Surfing is done where there are large **waves**. Surfers take their **surfboards** out and ride the waves back. There is a whole subculture of surfing, with a special vocabulary for the kinds of waves, the surfer's maneuvers, and the degree of difficulty of the ride.

  Snorkeling is done where there are (usually tropical) fish or coral structures that are beautiful and colorful up close underwater. Snorkelers wear **masks** that cover the eyes and nose, **snorkels** (which are tubes with mouthpieces at one end), and **flippers** on their feet. The snorkeler breathes through his/her mouth through the snorkel, the open end of which usually stays above the water's surface.

Scuba (*s*elf *c*ontained *u*nderwater *b*reathing *a*pparatus) gear allows divers to stay underwater for protracted lengths of time. Scuba divers must be certified. They wear **wet suits** (also worn by surfers in cooler weather), masks, flippers, and **scuba tanks**, which supply the diver with air.

Suggested Activities

1. Have the students describe the scene in as much detail as they can. For example, "The lifeguard is wearing a white T-shirt, red shorts, and a visor. She is standing on the platform of the lifeguard's chair, and is holding binoculars. She is about to blow her whistle because one of the swimmers has gone out too far. . . "

2. Have the students talk about any experiences they have had at the beach, real or imaginary, including the name of the beach, who they were with, what kind of day (weather) it was, what they did, etc.

92 Team Sports

Notes About the Dictionary Page

This page illustrates close-ups of the players of the major team sports. More information on baseball and football is on page 93.

Cross-Reference

Sports (93–97)

Supplemental Vocabulary

inning	overtime
half	foul
quarter	equipment

Usage Notes

The term **football** is used around the world to refer to soccer, while the game played in the United States and Canada is called American football.

Culture Notes

- **Team sports** are played in high schools and colleges. Some, like **baseball**, football, **ice hockey**, and **basketball**, are played professionally. Team sports are also played in parks, schoolyards, and gyms by youth and adults in informal or organized fashion.

- There are youth leagues in many sports for boys and girls of various ages, such as **Little League Baseball**, Pop Warner Football, and American Youth Soccer Organization Soccer.

- *Professional* team sports are played by men only. With high school and college sports, the sport determines whether women have teams or not. Baseball is played by men only; softball is played by women only. Football is played by men only. Ice hockey is almost always played by men only. **Lacrosse**, basketball, **volleyball**, and **soccer** are played by women and men.

- It is traditional to begin games in the United States with the playing of "The Star-Spangled Banner."

Resource Notes

The coach (93) of the team helps the players prepare physically and mentally for games. (In baseball and softball, the coach is called the *manager*.) The players on the team occupy different *positions*, and the number of players on the team depends on the sport. All teams have regular players and substitutes.

Playing Field	No. of Players	Playing Field	No. of Players
baseball diamond	9	ice hockey rink	6
softball diamond	10	basketball court	5
soccer field	11	volleyball court	6
lacrosse field	10	football field	11 (on the field at one time)

Sport	How Points Are Scored
baseball (and **softball**)	A *run* is scored when a runner touches all four bases: first base, second base, third base, and home plate.
football	*Points* are scored when a player gets the **football** (by running, catching, or kicking the ball) across the opponent's goal line.
lacrosse	A *goal* is scored when a player throws the ball from the lacrosse stick into the opponent's netted **goal**.
ice hockey	A goal is scored when a player shoots a **puck** into the other team's goal.
basketball	Points are scored when a player shoots the **basketball** into the opponent's basket.
volleyball	A point is scored by the serving team when the **volleyball** touches the floor inbounds on the opponent's side.
soccer	A goal is scored when a player kicks the **soccer ball** into the opponent's goal.

Suggested Activities

1. Have the students create a chart of the sport in one column, the number of players in another column, the kind of playing field in the third column, and the equipment used in the sport in the fourth, using the vocabulary listed and any additional words you have given.

2. Have the students ask each other questions beginning with "Which sport?" such as, "Which sport uses a puck?" or "Which sport is played on a diamond?" etc.

3. Have the students write a sentence to describe the action in each of the pictures in the illustration.

93 Ballfields

Notes About the Dictionary Page

The list of football players on this page includes only the offensive positions. Defensive positions and special teams players are included below.

Cross-Reference

Sports (92, 96–97)

Culture Notes

• **Baseball** and **football** are considered national pastimes. *Fans* get very involved in *rooting* for their favorite *teams*, which are often the teams that play in a *stadium* geographically close to them. Teams are referred to by their locations and team names, such as the San Francisco Giants and the Houston Oilers.

• When the team plays in its own stadium, it is the *home team* and plays *at home*. The other team is the *visiting team*, and plays *away*. Often the same stadium is shared by the football team and the baseball team since there are only one or two months of overlap in the baseball and football seasons. Some stadiums are enclosed with *domes*; many now have artificial turf.

- Individuals and corporations buy tickets to games; especially in football, it is usual for the tickets to all the games in a season to be sold as a *season ticket*. In some communities, the games are sold out to season ticket holders and there are waiting lists that are years long.

- Watching sports at home is equally as popular as being at the stadium, and there are advantages in viewing the game from close-up cameras. *Instant replays* are videotaped playbacks of plays that have just taken place. *Spectators* and *home viewers* like to see the play again, either because the play was exciting or because something questionable occurred.

Notes on A

- Major league baseball has two *leagues*, the American League and the National League, both of which are further divided into the Eastern and Western *divisions*. Baseball is played from April to October. The two teams that have the best record in each division at the end of the season play each other in the *playoffs*, and the winner receives the *pennant*. These two teams then play each other in the *World Series*, which is won by the first team to win four games out of a possible seven.

- The object of baseball is for one team to score more *runs* than the other team. A baseball game has nine *innings*. Each team gets a turn to *score* during each inning, and there is no time limit for a game. If the score is tied, or if there is no score after nine innings, extra innings are played.

  A run is scored when a player advances around all four **bases** and crosses **home plate.** He does this by hitting the ball out of reach of the opposing team players. If this is done on a single hit, it is called a *home run*. Games are played all week long, both during the day and at night. A *doubleheader* is two games played back-to-back between the same opponents. If the weather becomes too inclement, the game is *rained out*.

Supplemental Vocabulary

error	strike	single	fly ball
runs batted in	strike out	double	foul ball
count	stolen bases	triple	tag
ball	infield	double play	pinstripes (uniform)
walk	outfield	side is retired	bullpen

Culture Notes

- The first game of the season is always held in Cincinnati, the home of the oldest baseball team (the Cincinnati Reds). The Commissioner of Baseball "throws out the first ball." The President of the United States or another important public figure throws out the first ball at the World Series games.

- The umpire yells, "Play ball!" at the start of the game.

- The song "Take Me Out to the Ball Game" is an old, popular song often played during the "seventh inning stretch." (Take me out to the ball game/Take me out to the crowd/Buy me some peanuts and Cracker Jack/I don't care if I never get back/For it's root, root, root for the home team/If they don't win, it's a shame/For it's one, two, three strikes, you're out, in the old ball game.)

Notes on B

- Professional football has one league, the National Football League (NFL). There are two *conferences*, or associations of teams, the National Football Conference and the American Football Conference, both of which have Eastern, Central, and Western Divisions. Football is played from September to January. The best team in the National Conference plays the best team in the American Conference in the *Super Bowl*, a single game, which is watched all over the world by millions of people.

- Football is the only game where there are two separate teams within the team, one for *offensive play* and one for *defensive play*. The defensive alignment includes 11 players: four *linemen* (two defensive **tackles** and two defensive **ends**), three *linebackers*, two *cornerbacks*, and two *safeties*. In addition, each team has players on *special teams*—punter, place kicker, holder, and punt receiver—for such plays as *punts*, *field goals*, and *kickoffs*.

- The object of the game is for one team to score more points than the other. The football field is 100 yards long. Each end has a *goal line* and an **end zone.**

  Each team gets four downs to advance the ball at least 10 yards. If the team is unable to do so, the opposing team takes possession of the ball. Officials on the field may call penalties against a team if it has violated any rules of the game. Total playing time is 60 minutes, divided up into quarters. The first half is separated from the second half by a 15-minute intermission, called *halftime*.

  Points are scored in a number of ways, the most common of which is the *touchdown*, when the players on one team get the ball across the opponent's goal line into their end zone. A touchdown is six points. After the touchdown is made, the team gets a chance to score an *extra point* by kicking the ball from the opponent's 20-yard line between the **goalposts.** (In college football, the team can score two extra points if the ball is run or passed into the end zone instead of kicked.) The team may score a field goal (three points) by kicking the ball between the opponent's goalposts from anywhere on the field, but usually between the 50- and 20-yard lines. The defensive team scores a *safety* (two points) if a player on the offensive team is tackled in his own end zone.

Culture Notes

Most football games are played on Sundays. (College games are also very popular, and are usually played on Saturdays.) Games are played in any weather. During football season, wives who do not themselves watch the games, but whose husbands do, are called "football widows."

Supplemental Vocabulary

first down	lateral	time-out	fumble
first and ten	shoulder pads	penalty	loose ball
formation	jersey	the snap	blocking
pigskin	numbers	huddle	sidelines
pass	fair catch	touchback	sudden-death overtime
forward pass	line of scrimmage		

- officials: referee; line judge; field judge; back judge; side judge; umpire

Suggested Activities

1. Have the students research the answers to the following questions by talking to native speakers: Which two teams played in the latest World Series? Who won? How many games in total were played during the series? Which two teams played in the latest Super Bowl? Who won? What was the score?

2. Have the students interview a fan of a baseball or football team to find out which player the fan likes most and why. The students can interview each other if they are fans.

3. Have the students describe a game played in their native country.

94 Individual Sports

Notes About the Dictionary Page	This page gives a glimpse of a variety of individual sports. Page 95 has additional information on tennis, golf, skiing, and horse racing.
Cross-Reference	*Sports (92–93, 95–97) Other sports: biking (52), fishing (88), swimming (90)*
Alternate Words	**Ping-Pong** table tennis
Resource Notes	Most of the sports on this page can be done for *competition* and *recreation*; a few, like **horse racing**, **boxing**, and **gymnastics**, are competitive sports only. Many of the sports pictured are favorite *spectator sports*. While all the sports pictured are **individual sports**, some can involve teammates; **tennis** can be played as doubles, **ice skating** can be in pairs, and **track and field** includes relay racing.
Notes on Tennis	See notes on Fields and Courses (Guide 115).
Notes on Bowling	The objective in **bowling** is to knock down the ten bowling **pins** given two throws of the **bowling ball** in each of ten *frames* of the game. The ten pins are arranged with one in the front (the headpin), two in the second row, three in the third, and four in the fourth. If all the pins are knocked down on the first throw, the bowler has a *strike*. If all the pins are knocked down on the first two throws, the bowler has a *spare*. The maximum score a bowler can get is 300 points, the *score* obtained when all ten frames are strikes.
Notes on Golf	See notes on Fields and Courses (Guide 116).
Notes on Handball	The objective in **handball** is to score more *points* than the *opponent*. Points are scored by the person serving when the opponent misses a shot. If the server misses a shot, the opponent takes over the serve. The ball used in handball is small and hard with little bounce.
Notes on Boxing	The objective in boxing is to knock down the opponent. The two fighters occupy different corners of the **ring**. A match is usually ten *rounds*, with each round lasting three minutes. If there is no *knockout* (KO), or *technical knockout* (TKO), then the winner is determined on the basis of points awarded by the judges (*decision*).
Notes on Ping-Pong	The objective in **Ping-Pong** is to score more points than the opponent, according to the same rules as handball. The **ping-pong ball** is a small, white, hollow ball made of translucent celluloid or plastic.
Notes on Horse Racing	See notes on Fields and Courses (Guide 116).
Notes on Gymnastics	Men's and women's gymnastics have different *exercises*. Men's gymnastics includes the parallel bars, the pommel horse, the still rings, the vault, and floor routines. Women's gymnastics includes the uneven bars, the **balance beam**, the vault, and floor routines. The best score that can be obtained for any exercise is a ten.
Notes on Ice Skating	Ice skating can mean *speed skating* or *figure skating*. Speed skating is similar to foot racing. Figure skating includes "school figures," such as figure eights, and free skating, which includes various steps, turns, and jumps. The best score that can be obtained for any routine is a ten.

**Notes on
Racquetball**

The objective in **racquetball** is to score more points than the opponent, according to the same rules as handball. A racquetball court has four walls. The **racquetball** is a very bouncy, fairly large, blue, rubber ball, and the **racquet** has a relatively large face. *Squash* is similar to racquetball, but is played on a smaller court, with a black, hard, rubber ball, and a small-faced, long-handled racquet.

**Notes on
Track and Field**

Track and field is both an indoor and outdoor sport made up of several *events*: running, pole-vaulting, broad-jumping, etc. Among the running events are dashes, relay races, and hurdles.

**Notes on Cross-
Country Skiing**

Cross-country skiing is snow skiing done on relatively flat land, as opposed to *downhill (alpine) skiing,* which is done on *ski slopes. Nordic skiing* and *ski touring* are other names for cross-country skiing. The **skis** used for cross-country skiing are much narrower and longer than downhill skis, and are worn with cross-country shoes instead of boots; the **poles** are much longer than those used in downhill skiing. More information on downhill skiing is on Guide 116.

**Suggested
Activities**

1. Have the students ask each other questions beginning with "Which sport?" such as, "Which sport uses a racket?" or "Which sport is played in a ring?"

2. Have the students write a sentence to describe the action in each of the pictures in the illustration.

3. Have the students talk about any sport they have participated in or would like to participate in, either as an athlete or spectator. What was their experience? Were they good at the game/sport? If appropriate, provide a model from your own experience.

95 Fields and Courses

Cross-Reference

Sports (92–94, 96–97)

**Notes on Tennis
Court**

- **Tennis** is both a recreational and competitive sport.

  It is played on a **tennis court** whose surface may be clay, grass, synthetic, or concrete. If the *match* is played by two people, it is called *singles*, and the singles court is used (the boundaries of the court are reduced by four and a half feet on either side—the *alleys*). If the match is played by four people, it is called *doubles*, and the full court is used.

  Scoring in tennis is unique. Regardless of who is serving, both players can score points. A score of "0" is called *love*. The first point scored is 15, the next 30, the next 40, and then *game*. The first player to win six games wins the *set*. The first player to win two out of three or three out of five sets wins the match.

- **Professional tennis** is an international sport. U.S. players belong to the United States Tennis Association (USTA). Players are *ranked* by a computer ranking system. The top players are seeded, with the number one player being first *seed*. The most important *tennis tournament* in this country is the U.S. Open, which is held in late summer in Flushing Meadow, NY. Internationally, the most important tennis tournament is Wimbledon, which is held in early summer in Wimbledon, England.

Notes on Golf Course

- **Golf** is both a recreational and competitive sport.

  It is played on a **golf course** that has 18 *holes*. Each golf course is designed with a number of hazards, such as **sand traps** and water hazards, between the *tee* and the *cup*, which is marked with a **flag**. Since courses vary in difficulty, *par*, the standard number of *strokes* it takes a golfer to complete the course, varies from course to course. The golfer's objective is to complete the course in as few strokes as possible, and total scores for professionals are in terms relative to par, as in "five below par," "two above par." Recreational golfers give their scores as the total number of strokes, such as 86 or 104.

  The golfer has a set of golf **clubs**, which include *irons, woods*, and a putter (94). The selection of a club is determined by the kind of shot the golfer is trying to make. The golfer tees off—sets the golf ball on the tee, addresses the ball, and drives it toward the hole. If the ball goes in in one shot, it is called a *hole-in-one*.

- **Professional golf** is an international sport. U.S. players belong to the Professional Golf Association (PGA) or the Ladies Professional Golf Association (LPGA). The Masters Tournament is the most prestigious tournament played in this country.

Notes on Ski Slope

- *Downhill skiing* is a recreational and competitive sport.

  People go skiing for a day, for a weekend or they take ski vacations. Those who ski often own their own equipment—**ski boots, bindings, skis**, and **poles**—but it is possible to rent equipment from a ski shop. **Ski slopes** are rated for beginner, intermediate, advanced, and expert. **Ski lifts** transport skiers from the base of the slope to the top.

- Famous *ski resorts* are located in the Rocky Mountain States, New England, the Pacific Northwest, northern California, and the northern Mid-Atlantic States.

- As a competitive sport, there is free-form skiing and racing—downhill racing, slalom, and giant slalom skiing. The difference among the kinds of racing is related to the number of turns the skier must make.

Notes on Race Track

- Horse racing is a competitive sport. There is *thoroughbred racing* and *harness racing* (trotters). People go to the **race track** to watch the races and to bet on the horses, since betting is legal at the track. In some states, there is government sponsored off-track betting.

  The horse that crosses the **finish line** first wins the race. If the race is close, the results are determined by examining a photo, and it is known as a *photo finish*. A horse can win by a nose, a neck, a length, etc.

- The best-known thoroughbred races in the United States are the Kentucky Derby, the Preakness, and the Belmont Stakes. Together, they make up the *Triple Crown*.

Suggested Activities

1. Have the students ask each other questions beginning with "Which sport?" such as, "Which sport uses a racket?" or "Which sport is played on a court?"

2. Have the students write a sentence to describe the action in each of the pictures in the illustration.

3. Have the students interview a person who plays tennis or golf, who skis, or who likes horse racing to find out what he/she likes most about the sport. The students can interview each other if appropriate.

96 & 97 Sports Verbs

Notes About the Dictionary Page
There are two illustrations for most of the verbs on these pages. The verbs illustrated on this page are presented in the context of sports, but may be used in a variety of contexts in our speech.

Cross-Reference
Sports (92–95)

Language Notes

hit/hit/hit	**fall**/fell/fallen	**dive**/dove (dived)/dived
catch/caught/caught	**throw**/threw/thrown	**drive**/drove/driven
run/ran/run	**ride**/rode/ridden	

Most of these verbs are transitive, with the exception of run, fall, jump, skate, surf, and dive. Bounce can be transitive or intransitive, as in "He bounced the ball," and "The ball bounced."

Resource Notes

Verb	Sports
hit	baseball, tennis, football, boxing, golf
serve	tennis, volleyball, Ping-Pong, racquetball
kick	soccer, football
catch	baseball, lacrosse, softball, football, basketball
pass	basketball, ice hockey, football, lacrosse, soccer
run	baseball, track and field, softball, basketball, tennis
fall	basketball, soccer, gymnastics, boxing, ice skating, skiing
jump	basketball, rope, football, track and field, ice skating, skiing
skate	ice skating, roller skating, ice hockey, figure skating
throw	baseball, darts, boxing, racquetball, football
bounce	basketball, tennis, racquetball, Ping-Pong
surf	surfing, body surfing, wind sailing
ride	horseback riding, biking
dive	diving, scuba diving, football
drive	auto racing, football, golf
shoot	basketball, archery

Suggested Activities

1. Have the students list all the sports pictured on pages 92–95 in one column. In the next column, ask them to list as many verbs as they can to go along with each sport. Provide examples to get them started, if appropriate.

2. Have the students take turns pantomiming a verb of their choosing, relative to any sport they like, and have the other students guess what verb and what sport are being pantomimed.

3. Have the students make up two sentences about each illustration using two different verb tenses. For example, "The batter hit a home run," and "The tennis player won't hit the ball."

98 Musical Instruments

Cross-Reference	*Music (99)*		

Supplemental Vocabulary	English horn	rehearsal	play
	orchestra	concert	sing
	band	performance	tune

Alternate Words	**violin**	fiddle
	saxophone	sax

Culture Notes

Music study is very popular in the United States, and many people learn to play one or more instruments for pleasure. Students also join *bands, orchestras*, and *choruses* in school, and high school students can enter competitions to play in district, state, and national groups. People can study with the teachers at their school, or they can study privately with someone who is particularly skilled on their instrument.

Resource Notes

Musical instruments are divided into three broad classes: the **strings**, which all have strings that are plucked or bowed; the *winds*, which are sounded by the breath; and the **percussion** instruments, which are hammered or struck.

Instrument	*Distinguishing Features*
String Instruments	
piano	has *hammers* that are operated from a **keyboard** and strike upon metal **strings**; also categorized as a percussion instrument
ukelele	guitarlike Hawaiian instrument with four strings that are plucked or strummed with the fingers
mandolin	has (usually) metal strings that are plucked with a plectrum
banjo	a guitarlike instrument with long fretted neck and five metal strings that are plucked or strummed with the fingers
harp	the strings are stretched between the soundbox and the neck and are plucked with the fingers; come in many sizes; angels in Heaven are often pictured playing harps
violin	a four-stringed instrument, held nearly horizontal by the player's arm with the lower portion supported against the collarbone or shoulder; played with a **bow** or plucked
viola	slightly larger than the violin; played like a violin
cello	also called violincello; the third largest member of the violin family; it rests vertically on the floor between the (seated) performer's knees when being played
bass	also called *bass fiddle, double bass*; the largest instrument of the violin family; it rests vertically on the floor when being played; performer stands or leans back on high stool to play
guitar	has a long, fretted neck, (usually) six strings; it is plucked or strummed with fingers or a **pick**

Wind Instruments (Woodwinds and Brass)

piccolo	a **woodwind**; a small flute sounding an octave higher than a regular flute
flute	a woodwind; a tube with a series of fingerholes or *keys* played by a flautist (or flutist)
bassoon	a large woodwind of low range; has a double-*reed mouthpiece*
oboe	a woodwind with a double-reed mouthpiece; orchestras tune from the oboe's pitch
clarinet	a woodwind with a single reed attached to its mouthpiece
trombone	a **brass** wind instrument; has a cylindrical metal tube that expands into a *bell* and bends twice in a U-shape; usually equipped with a *slide*
saxophone	a brass wind instrument; has a conical, usually brass tube with keys or valves and a mouthpiece with one reed
trumpet	a brass wind instrument that has a tube commonly curved one or twice around on itself; has a cup-shaped mouthpiece at one end and a flaring bell at the other
French horn	a brass wind instrument that has a long, coiled tube
tuba	a *valved* brass wind instrument that has a very low range
accordion	a portable wind instrument with a large *bellows* and keys that operate small metal reeds
organ	has one or more sets of *pipes* sounded by means of compressed air; played by means of one or more keyboards
harmonica	contains a set of metal reeds connected to a row of holes, over which the player places his mouth and produces sounds by inhaling and exhaling

Percussion Instruments

tambourine	a small drum that has several pairs of disks on its circular frame; played by shaking or striking against the hand
cymbal	concave plate of brass or bronze; played in pairs by striking together or singly by striking with a **drumstick**
drum	has a hollow, (usually) cylindrical body with a membrane stretched over one or both ends; played by striking with the hand, a stick, or a pair of sticks
conga	a tall, narrow-headed bass drum beaten with the hands
kettledrum	a drum of brass or copper; the tension of its skin can be modified with hand screws or foot pedals
bongos	a pair of small, tuned drums played by beating with the fingers
xylophone	has a graduated series of wooden bars usually sounded by striking with a wooden hammer

1. Bring in recordings of solo instrumental pieces and have the students listen to the sounds produced by such instruments as the piano, guitar, violin, saxophone, clarinet, etc.

2. Write the words "strings," "winds," and "percussions" on separate areas of the chalkboard, and write all the musical instruments on the page on separate index cards. Have the students pick a card, say the name of the instrument, and tape it under the correct heading on the board.

3. Ask the students if they play an instrument and, if so, what kind. Discuss whether it is one that is in the Dictionary or not.

99 Music, Dance, and Theater

**Notes About the
Dictionary Page**

The ballet illustrated is probably being performed at a big theater in a large city. The theater shown here would also house an orchestra, opera performances, and touring companies. Most musical comedies are done in smaller, Broadway-style houses. The rock group is probably performing in a small club.

Cross-Reference

Instruments (98)

**Supplemental
Vocabulary**

musicals	act	backstage	microphone
conduct	perform	downstage	cue
direct	dance	upstage	sing

Alternate Words

| **scenery** | sets |
| **spotlight** | spot |

Usage Notes

- People often go to the movies. We say, "go to the movies," but we see "a movie." Movies play at movie theaters.

- Theater people who want to wish someone good luck say, "Break a leg."

- When performers take their bows and acknowledge the audience's applause at the end of a *play*, *musical*, or *opera*, they take their "curtain call."

Culture Notes

- *Entertainment* is a large and popular industry in the United States, and performers are often *celebrities*. "Going out" to see a show or a concert is a social event for many people. Couples use shows and movies as the focus of a *date*.

- **Music, dance, and theater** are broad categories for the variety of *performances* people attend. The performances may be by *professional* companies or by local, *amateur* acting companies in large performing arts centers, on *Broadway* or its equivalent in other cities outside of New York, in colleges and universities, and in parks.

- *Touring companies* are groups that perform all over the country. Most Broadway shows have a touring company, even while the Broadway cast is still performing. Other groups, like *ballet troupes*, will go on tour for several months each year. Touring companies perform "on the road."

Resource Notes

- The formal physical theater has a **stage**, a **curtain**, **scenery**, *footlights*, **spotlights**, and an *orchestra pit*. Seating for the audience is usually **orchestra, mezzanine, balcony**, and **box seats**, with the ticket price highest for orchestra and box seats. Tickets can be purchased at the *box office* (in person or by mail) or through an electronic ticket vendor for a service charge. *Twofers* are passes that allow you to buy two tickets for the price of one. *Matinees* are afternoon performances, usually on Wednesdays and Saturdays at 2 P.M. Evening performances are usually at 8 P.M.

- **Musical comedies**, plays, and operas are staged by a *director*, who plans all the *blocking* (stage movement) and coaches the performers in their parts. *Producers* put up the money for the costs of a show. All the performers in a show make up the *cast*, and the people who do the technical work of the production are the *crew*. *Stagehands* are the people who move the scenery for each scene of a show. After weeks or months of *rehearsal*, a show opens, and the first night is called *opening night*. The show then has a "run" and closes.

- *Lyricists* write the words for a musical comedy or an opera, and *composers* write music. Plays are written by *playwrights*, while *choreographers* create dances.

- **Rock** music can vary from "soft" pop-rock to "heavy-metal" music. Rock groups perform everywhere from *clubs* to large *stadiums*. People who work on setting up a band's equipment for a show are called *roadies*, since they travel with the band.

- Types of Live Performances:
  Music—Concerts and Recitals: symphony orchestras, chamber music orchestras, rock groups (or other kinds of groups: country, rhythm and blues, etc.), individual performers

  Opera: Classical operas, Light operas, Rock operas

  Dance: Classical ballet, Modern dance, Folk dance, Ethnic dance

  Theater—Plays: comedy, drama; Musicals: comedy, drama; Improvisation

  Shows: Magic shows, Revues

Suggested Activities

1. Bring in the entertainment section from the local Sunday newspaper. Have each student pick out something he/she would like to see, and have each student write a mock letter to the box office. Give the students a model letter requesting tickets, including the date and time of the performance, the number of tickets, the kind of seating, the amount of the check enclosed, etc.

2. If the students have gone to any music, dance, or theatrical performances in the United States, have them tell the class about their experience.

3. If the students go to the movies, have each one review the last movie he/she attended, without giving away plot details.

100 Electronics and Photography

Notes About the Dictionary Page

The top half of Picture A illustrates a mother using a video camera and Minicam to videotape her husband and their infant daughter, who is taking her first steps. The lower half of the picture shows the tape being played back on their TV through their VCR. (Note that videocameras and Minicams are no longer being marketed; they have been replaced by single-unit camcorders that are less cumbersome and lighter in weight.)

Picture B shows a 35-mm, single-lens-reflex (SLR) camera on a tripod. Film may be color or black and white, for slides or prints, and of varying speeds for indoor or outdoor use. Picture C illustrates a camerawoman using a professional movie camera on a movie set. Movie technology, while used commercially, is being replaced by videotapes for home use. Picture D shows an assortment of stereo audio equipment. The young man is listening to either a cassette or AM/FM radio on his Walkman. Picture E illustrates both a personal computer—also called a PC—and a hand calculator.

Alternate Words

videocassette   videotapes/tapes/videos

Usage Notes

Stereo system is a general term for various combinations of a **turntable, receiver, cassette deck**, and **speakers**. People refer to the entire system as a *stereo*.

Culture Notes

The technological revolution has affected the average household. People can now afford **electronic** equipment that was once very expensive. Many devices have changed people's lifestyles by saving time, allowing greater freedom, and providing new forms of entertainment.

Notes on A

- **Videocassette recorders (VCRs)** allow you to do several things. With a **video camera** and **Minicam** or with a *camcorder* (all-in-one unit), you can make your own **videocassettes**. These have replaced home movies for many people (see Notes on C). With a programmable *timer*, you can program your VCR to record something while you are out or while you are watching another channel so you can watch it at another time. People no longer have to miss favorite shows or arrange their schedules around the **television**. You can also record something special and save it to watch again and again. You can rent or buy videos and see movies at home not long after their commercial runs without going to the movies. And you can rent or buy videos that teach you how to do something or that have other educational value.

- Televisions have become both smaller and larger. Screens range in size from an inch and a half to six feet. *TVs* are available in stereo, with VCRs built in, and with remote controls (28). It is common for one household to have more than one TV.

Notes on B

Photography is both a *hobby* for people and a way of recording memories. For those who are not photography buffs, camera companies are making **cameras** that do not require much skill to use, with such features as auto(matic) focus, auto advance/rewind, auto film exposure, built-in **flash**, built-in self-timer, etc.

Notes on C

Many families take *home movies*, especially of children during their infancy and early childhood. Movies are taken with **movie cameras**, and the film must be sent away to be developed. You need a movie **projector** to show the movies and a movie **screen** (or a blank wall). With the advent of camcorders, many people have begun to make videocassettes instead of taking home movies. It is possible also to have films converted into videos, so old home movies can be shown using VCRs.

Notes on D

There are a number of choices available when it comes to **audio** systems for playing prerecorded music. For your home, you can get a turntable to play records (albums, LPs, 45s), or you can get a cassette deck to play (audio)**cassettes**, or you can get a **compact disc player** to play **compact discs** (**CDs**), which are based on laser technology. All of these components play through the stereo receiver, which is a combination of an amplifier and a tuner (radio). Most cars come with a radio (50), and you can get a cassette player or CD player in addition. For walking around, you can get a lightweight (**Sony Walkman**-type) AM/FM stereo radio/cassette player with **headphones** or a heavy **stereo cassette player** (ghetto blaster, boom box).

Notes on E

- Today's **personal computers** have the power that large computers had in the 1970s. They are used in the home for business applications (such as bookkeeping, financial forecasting, and stock market analysis), word processing, and video games. Although computers do calculations, hand **calculators** are common for everyday calculations, such as balancing your checkbook.

- *Phone answering machines* are common devices and are used to screen calls as well as to record messages while you are out.

Suggested Activities

1. Have the students categorize the appropriate items on the page according to the following headings: things that take pictures, things that show pictures, things that record music, things that play music, and things that do calculations.

2. Have each student bring in a picture of a piece of electronic equipment from an ad in a magazine, newspaper, or department store sales catalog. In pairs, they then roleplay the customer and salesperson in an electronics store, using the picture as a prop.

3. Have the students make up a story about the people in Pictures A, C, and E, using the vocabulary listed and any additional words you have given.

101 Handicrafts

Cross-Reference

Clothes (19–24)

Notes on A

- People sew to create new items, such as clothing, curtains, and gifts, as well as to fix or alter things. **Sewing machines** are controlled by a foot or knee pedal. There is a **spool of thread** at the top, and a spool of thread (*bobbin*) right below the plate under the needle. **Stitches** are formed by the action of the threaded needle catching the bobbin thread to create a running stitch.

  Generally, most modern sewing machines do all types of stitches, many of which used to be done by hand. Some people still do *basting* and **hems** by hand.

- When sewing from a **pattern**, you have to lay out the **pattern pieces**. Cutting the pattern out with **pinking shears** keeps the cut edges from raveling. You transfer special marks (darts, sewing lines, **buttonholes**) from the pattern onto the **material** (fabric).

You put in the **zipper** and sew the **seams** with the machine. After most of the machine sewing is done, you have to finish off the garment, sewing on **buttons**, putting in **snaps**, and sewing **hooks and eyes**, if these closures are appropriate. The last thing to be done is the hem. Usually you machine sew the **hem binding** to the garment, then do a blind hem stitch. You protect your finger from the back of the needle with a **thimble** when you push the needle through.

Notes on B

- **Knitting** requires two **knitting needles** and **wool** or other **yarn**. There are two basic stitches in knitting, *knit* and *purl*, from which various combinations produce different patterns and textures. Sweaters and scarves are often hand knit.

- **Needlepoint**, or *tapestry*, involves a mesh design, threaded yarn, and a single kind of stitch. **Embroidery** may be *crewel* work, which uses a variety of stitches and crewel yarn, or *cross stitch*, which uses cotton embroidery thread and stitches in the shape of crosses. Needlepoint and crewel work are typically done on wall hangings and seat covers, while cross stitch is typically done on tablecloths, hand towels, and crib accessories.

- **Crochet** can be done with cotton, wool, or other yarn. When you crochet, you use one **crochet hook** and form loops of yarn with your other hand to make the basic stitch. Afghan blankets and doilies are often crocheted by hand.

- **Weaving** is done with a hand **loom**; yarn wound on a shuttle becomes the threads of the woof when interwoven with the threads of the warp on the loom.

- **Quilting** involves three layers: the top is made of squares (or other shapes) of fabric sewn together; the middle is batting; and the bottom is plain fabric. After the three layers are sewn together around the edges, the quilter sews on the squares through all the layers, attaching the layers throughout the quilt, and creating a stitched design on both sides, starting from the center, going out to each corner and then to the top and bottom and two sides.

Suggested Activities

1. Bring in as many of the items on the list as possible. Have the students take turns picking up an item for the other students to name.

2. If any of the students do any handicrafts, have them bring in something they are working on and tell the class about it.

102 Prepositions of Description

Notes About the Dictionary Page

This page depicts prepositions of description, or static prepositions. These are used to indicate a state or position. Each cat on the page illustrates a preposition, as in "(the orange and white cat is) at (the window)." Page 103 illustrates prepositions of motion, which are used to indicate different aspects of motion.

Cross-Reference

Prepositions (103)

Resource Notes

It is difficult for learners of English to master the use of prepositions. To help them internalize the meaning and uses of the prepositions presented on this page, it is recommended that you provide a variety of activities, such as those listed below.

Suggested Activities

1. For each of the prepositions, have one student ask a question beginning with "Where's the?" such as, "Where's the cat with the red yarn in its mouth?" The other students say or write the answer, "It's behind the chair."

2. Give the students 11 index cards each and have them put their name on each card. Say one of the prepositions on the list. Give the students one minute to write a sentence using that preposition with the objects around the classroom, one sentence to a card. (See Activity #3.) For example, if you say "in front of," they can write, "The plant is in front of the window."

3. Collect the index cards from the second activity and make sure the sentences are correct. (Work with the students on these sentences if there are errors as a separate activity.) Also, remove any cards that are exact duplicates. Put all the cards into a basket and mix them up. Pick out a card and ask the students to identify the object from its description. For example, "It's in front of the window." The students have to say "the plant." Note that there may be more than one correct answer.

4. For each of the following Dictionary pages, have the students write descriptive sentences using as many prepositions from the list as possible:

Page	Topic	Page	Topic
14–15	The Supermarket	33	The Baby's Room
16	Family Restaurant and Cocktail Lounge	34	The Bathroom
		35	The Utility Room
20–21	Everyday Clothes	36–37	A Workshop
26	Seasonal Verbs	76	A Classroom
28	The Living Room	78	A Science Lab
29	The Dining Room	82	Construction
30	The Kitchen	83	An Office
32	The Bedroom	99	Music, Dance, and Theater

103 Prepositions of Motion

**Notes About the
Dictionary Page**
This page illustrates prepositions of motion, which are used to indicate different aspects of motion. Each golf ball on the page illustrates a preposition, as in "(the golf ball is going) through (the lighthouse)," except for items 9 and 10, in which cases the people illustrate the preposition. Page 102 illustrates prepositions of description, or static prepositions, which are used to indicate a state or position.

Cross-Reference
Prepositions (102)

Resource Notes
It is difficult for learners of English to master the use of prepositions. To help them internalize the meaning and uses of the prepositions presented on this page, it is recommended that you provide a variety of activities, such as those listed below.

**Suggested
Activities**

1. For each of the prepositions, have the students write a sentence describing the motion of the golf ball, such as "The woman in the yellow pants hit the golf ball through the lighthouse."

2. Ask a student to come to the front of the room. Demonstrate the preposition "around" by walking around the student at the front of the room. Ask the students to make up a sentence that describes your action using one of the prepositions on the list. A correct answer would be "(Teacher's name) is walking around (student's name)." Have each student pick one of the prepositions and figure out a way to illustrate it. Call each one up and have them whisper the idea to you so you can check its accuracy and feasibility. Then have each student demonstrate a preposition and the others make up sentences to describe his/her action.

3. For each of the following Dictionary pages, have the students write descriptive sentences using as many prepositions from the list as possible. For example (from page 39), "The girl with the cast is out of the wheelchair."

Page	Topic	Page	Topic
39	Medical and Dental Care	81	Farming and Ranching
44–45	The City	85	Occupations II
53	Highway Travel	87	Neighborhood Parks
54–55	Public Transportation	88–89	Outdoor Activities
56	Air Travel	90–91	At the Beach
59	Pleasure Boating	92	Team Sports
80	Energy	95	Fields and Courses

4. For the sentences generated in Activity 3, have the students write questions beginning with "What?" or "Who?" For example, "Who is out of the wheelchair?"

Appendix A
Countries of the World and Their Capital Cities
(by Continent)

North America

Note that some of the countries below are grouped as Central America, the Caribbean, and the West Indies.

Antigua and Barbuda	St. John's
The Bahamas	Nassau
Barbados	Bridgetown
Belize	Belmopan
Canada	Ottawa
Costa Rica	San José
Cuba	Havana
Dominica	Roseau
Dominican Republic	Santo Domingo
El Salvador	San Salvador
Grenada	St. George's
Guatemala	Guatemala City
Haiti	Port-au-Prince
Honduras	Tegucigalpa
Jamaica	Kingston
Mexico	Mexico City
Nicaragua	Managua
Panama	Panama
St. Christopher (St. Kitts) and Nevis	Basseterre
St. Lucia	Castries
St. Vincent and the Grenadines	Kingstown
Trinidad and Tobago	Port-of-Spain
United States	Washington, D. C.

South America

Argentina	Buenos Aires
Bolivia	Sucre/La Paz
Brazil	Brasília
Chile	Santiago
Colombia	Bogotá
Ecuador	Quito
Guyana	Georgetown
Paraguay	Asunción
Peru	Lima
Suriname	Paramaribo
Uruguay	Montevideo
Venezuela	Caracas

Europe

Note that some of the countries below are grouped as Western Europe, the Iberian Peninsula, the Low Countries, the Balkans, Scandinavia, and Eastern Europe.

Albania	Tirana
Andorra	Andorra la Vella
Austria	Vienna
Belgium	Brussels
Bulgaria	Sofia
Czechoslovakia	Prague
Denmark	Copenhagen
Federal Republic of Germany (West Germany)	Bonn
Finland	Helsinki
France	Paris
German Democratic Republic (East Germany)	East Berlin
Greece	Athens
Hungary	Budapest
Iceland	Reykjavik
Ireland	Dublin
Italy	Rome
Liechtenstein	Vaduz
Luxembourg	Luxembourg City
Malta	Valletta
Monaco	Monaco-Ville
Netherlands	Amsterdam
Norway	Oslo
Poland	Warsaw
Portugal	Lisbon
Romania	Bucharest
San Marino	San Marino
Spain	Madrid
Sweden	Stockholm
Switzerland	Bern
United Kingdom (England, Wales, Scotland, Northern Ireland, etc.)	London
Vatican City	Vatican City
Yugoslavia	Belgrade

Asia

Note that some of the countries below are grouped as the Middle East, the Near East, the Far East, Southern Asia, Southeastern Asia, and Indochina.

Afghanistan	Kabul
Bahrain	Manama
Bangladesh	Dacca
Bhutan	Thimphu
Brunei	Bandar Seri Begawan
Burma	Rangoon
China (Mainland)	Beijing
Cyprus	Nicosia
India	New Delhi
Indonesia	Jakarta
Iran	Tehran
Iraq	Baghdad
Israel	Jerusalem
Japan	Tokyo
Jordan	Amman
Kampuchea (Cambodia)	Phnom Penh
Korea, North	Pyongyang
Korea, South	Seoul
Kuwait	Kuwait
Laos	Vientiane
Lebanon	Beirut
Malaysia	Kuala Lumpur
Maldives	Male
Mongolia	Ulaanbaatar
Nepal	Kathmandu
Oman	Muscat
Pakistan	Islamabad
Philippines	Manila/Quezon City
Qatar	Doha
Saudi Arabia	Riyadh
Singapore	Singapore
Union of Soviet Socialist Republics (Soviet Union)	Moscow
Sri Lanka	Colombo
Syria	Damascus
Taiwan	Taipei
Thailand	Bangkok
Turkey	Ankara
United Arab Emirates	Abu Dhabi
Vietnam	Hanoi
Yemen, Arab Republic (North Yemen)	Sana'a
Yemen, Democratic (South Yemen)	Aden

Africa

Note that some of the countries below are grouped as Northern Africa, Southern Africa, Western Africa, and Eastern Africa.

Algeria	Algiers
Angola	Luanda
Benin	Porto-Novo
Botswana	Gaborone
Burkina Faso (Upper Volta)	Ouagadougou
Burundi	Bujumbura
Cameroon	Yaoundé
Cape Verde	Praia
Central African Republic	Bangui
Chad	N'Djamena
Comoros	Moroni
Congo	Brazzaville
Djibouti	Djibouti
Egypt	Cairo
Equatorial Guinea	Malabo
Ethiopia	Addis Ababa
Gabon	Libreville
The Gambia	Banjul
Ghana	Accra
Guinea	Conakry
Guinea-Bissau	Bissau
Ivory Coast	Abidjan
Kenya	Nairobi
Lesotho	Maseru
Liberia	Monrovia
Libya	Tripoli
Madagascar	Antananarivo
Malawi	Lilongwe
Mali	Bamako
Mauritania	Nouakchott
Mauritus	Port Louis
Morocco	Rabat
Mozambique	Maputo
Namibia (South-West Africa)	Windhoek
Niger	Niamey
Nigeria	Lagos
Rwanda	Kigali
São Tomé and Principe	São Tomé
Senegal	Dakar
Seychelles	Victoria
Sierra Leone	Freetown
Somalia	Mogadishu

(continued next page)

Appendix A
Countries of the World and Their Capital Cities
(by Continent)

Africa (continued)

South Africa	Pretoria/ Cape Town/ Bloemfontein
Sudan	Khartoum
Swaziland	Mbabane
Tanzania	Dar-es-Salaam
Togo	Lome
Tunisia	Tunis
Uganda	Kampala
Zaire	Kinshasa
Zambia	Lusaka
Zimbabwe	Harare

Australia

Australia	Canberra
New Zealand	Wellington
Papua New Guinea	Port Moresby

Nations of the Pacific

Fiji	Suva
Kiribati	Bairiki
Nauru	Yaren
Solomon Islands	Honiara
Tonga	Nuku'alofa
Tuvalu	Funafuti
Vanuatu	Port-Vila
Western Samoa	Apia

Colonies, Commonwealths, Territories, and Dependencies

These lands fall under the jurisdiction of another country (legal, political, military). The larger and more well known are listed with their capitals.

United Kingdom

Bermuda	Hamilton
British West Indies	

(Anguilla, British Virgin Islands, Cayman Islands, Monserrat, Turks and Caicos Islands)

Channel Islands	
Falkland Islands	Stanley
Gibraltar	
Hong Kong	Hong Kong

Colonies, Commonwealths, Territories, and Dependencies (continued)

Isle of Man	
Northern Ireland	Belfast

China

Tibet	Lhasa

Denmark

Greenland (Kalaallit Nunaat)	Gothab (Nuuk)

France

French Guiana	Cayenne
French Polynesia	Papeete
Guadaloupe	Basse-Terre
Martinique	Fort-de-France
Mayotte	
New Caledonia	Nouméa
Réunion	Saint Denis
St. Pierre and Miquelon	St. Pierre
Wallis and Futuna Islands	Mata-Utu

Netherlands

Aruba	
Netherlands Antilles	Willemstad

(Curaçao, Bonaire, St. Eustatius, St. Maarten, Saba)

Portugal

Macau	Macau

Spain

Balearic Islands	Palma

(Majorca, Minorca, Cabrera, Ibiza, Formentera)

Canary Islands	

United States

American Samoa	Pago Pago
Guam	Agana
Puerto Rico	San Juan
U.S. Trust Territory of the Pacific Islands (Micronesia) [Northern Mariana Islands, Federated States of Micronesia, Marshall Islands, Palau (Belau)]	
U.S. Virgin Islands	Charlotte Amalie

(St. John, St. Croix, St. Thomas)

Appendix B –The United States of America and its Capital Cities

(with abbreviations and date of entry into the Union)

State	Abbreviation		Capital	Date of Entry
Alabama	AL	Ala.	Montgomery	December 14, 1819
Alaska	AK	Alas.	Juneau	January 3, 1959
Arizona	AZ	Ariz.	Phoenix	February 14, 1912
Arkansas	AR	Ark.	Little Rock	June 15, 1836
California	CA	Cal./Calif.	Sacramento	September 9, 1850
Colorado	CO	Colo.	Denver	August 1, 1876
Connecticut	CT	Conn.	Hartford	January 9, 1788
Delaware	DE	Del.	Dover	December 7, 1787
Florida	FL	Fla.	Tallahassee	March 3, 1845
Georgia	GA		Atlanta	January 2, 1788
Hawaii	HI	Ha.	Honolulu	August 21, 1959
Idaho	ID	Ida.	Boise	July 3, 1890
Illinois	IL	Ill.	Springfield	December 3, 1818
Indiana	IN	Ind.	Indianapolis	December 11, 1816
Iowa	IA		Des Moines	December 28, 1846
Kansas	KS	Kan.	Topeka	January 29, 1861
Kentucky	KY		Frankfort	June 1, 1792
Louisiana	LA		Baton Rouge	April 30, 1812
Maine	ME		Augusta	March 15, 1820
Maryland	MD		Annapolis	April 28, 1788
Massachusetts	MA	Mass.	Boston	February 6, 1788
Michigan	MI	Mich.	Lansing	January 26, 1837
Minnesota	MN	Minn.	St. Paul	May 11, 1858
Mississippi	MS	Miss.	Jackson	December 10, 1817
Missouri	MO		Jefferson City	August 10, 1821
Montana	MT	Mon.	Helena	November 8, 1889
Nebraska	NB	Neb.	Lincoln	March 1, 1867
Nevada	NE	Nev.	Carson City	October 31, 1864
New Hampshire	NH		Concord	June 21, 1788
New Jersey	NJ		Trenton	December 18, 1787
New Mexico	NM		Santa Fe	January 6, 1912
New York	NY		Albany	July 26, 1788
North Carolina	NC		Raleigh	November 21, 1789
North Dakota	ND		Bismarck	November 2, 1889
Ohio	OH		Columbus	March 1, 1803
Oklahoma	OK	Okla.	Oklahoma City	November 16, 1907
Oregon	OR	Ore.	Salem	February 14, 1859
Pennsylvania	PA	Penn.	Harrisburg	December 12, 1787
Rhode Island	RI		Providence	May 29, 1790
South Carolina	SC		Columbia	May 23, 1788
South Dakota	SD		Pierre	November 2, 1889
Tennessee	TN	Tenn.	Nashville	June 1, 1796
Texas	TX	Tex.	Austin	December 29, 1845
Utah	UT		Salt Lake City	January 4, 1896
Vermont	VT		Montpelier	March 4, 1791
Virginia	VA		Richmond	June 25, 1788
Washington	WA	Wash.	Olympia	November 11, 1889
West Virginia	WV	W. Va.	Charleston	June 20, 1863
Wisconsin	WI	Wis.	Madison	May 29, 1848
Wyoming	WY		Cheyenne	July 10, 1890

Appendix C
Metric Conversion Tables

CONVERSION FROM METRIC MEASURES

Symbol	When You Know	Multiply By	To Find	Sym.
LENGTH				
cm	centimeters	0.393701	inches	in.
m	meters	3.280840	feet	ft.
m	meters	1.093613	yards	yd.
km	kilometers	0.621371	miles	mi.
MASS				
g	grams	0.035274	ounces	oz.
kg	kilograms	2.204623	pounds	lb.
VOLUME				
mL	milliliters	0.033814	liquid ounces	liq. oz.
L	liters	2.113376	pints	pt.
L	liters	1.056688	quarts	qt.
L	liters	0.264172	gallons	gal.

CONVERSION TO METRIC MEASURES

Symbol	When You Know	Multiply By	To Find	Sym.
LENGTH				
in.	inches	2.54	centimeters	cm
ft.	feet	0.3048	meters	m
yd.	yards	0.9144	meters	m
mi.	miles	1.609344	kilometers	km
MASS				
oz.	ounces	28.349523	grams	g
lb.	pounds	0.453592	kilograms	kg
VOLUME				
liq. oz.	liquid ounces	29.57353	milliliters	mL
pt.	pints	0.473176	liters	L
qt.	quarts	0.946353	liters	L
gal.	gallons	3.785412	liters	L

From *The National Geographic Atlas of the World*, page 235.
Copyright © 1981, The National Geographic Society.

Appendix D
United States Military Rankings

Army	Navy	Air Force	Marines
general of the Army	fleet admiral	general of the Air Force	
general	admiral	general	general
colonel	captain	colonel	colonel
major	lieutenant commander	major	major
captain	lieutenant	captain	captain
first lieutenant	lieutenant, junior grade	first lieutenant	first lieutenant
second lieutenant	ensign	second lieutenant	second lieutenant
first sergeant or master sergeant	senior chief petty officer	senior master sergeant	first sergeant or master sergeant
corporal or specialist 4	petty officer third class	sergeant	corporal
private	seaman recruit	airman basic	private

Appendix E
North American Professional Sports Teams

Baseball

National League
Atlanta Braves
Chicago Cubs
Cincinnati Reds
Houston Astros
Los Angeles Dodgers
Montreal Expos
New York Mets
Philadelphia Phillies
Pittsburgh Pirates
St. Louis Cardinals
San Diego Padres
San Francisco Giants

American League
Baltimore Orioles
Boston Red Sox
California Angels
Chicago White Sox
Cleveland Indians
Detroit Tigers
Kansas City Royals
Milwaukee Brewers
Minnesota Twins
New York Yankees
Oakland A's
Seattle Mariners
Texas Rangers
Toronto Blue Jays

Football

National Football League
Atlanta Falcons
Buffalo Bills
Chicago Bears
Cincinnati Bengals
Cleveland Browns
Dallas Cowboys
Denver Broncos
Detroit Lions
Green Bay Packers
Houston Oilers
Indianapolis Colts
Kansas City Chiefs
Los Angeles Raiders
Miami Dolphins
Minnesota Vikings
New England Patriots
New Orleans Saints
New York Giants
New York Jets
Philadelphia Eagles
Pittsburgh Steelers
St. Louis Cardinals
San Diego Chargers
San Francisco 49ers
Seattle SeaHawks
Tampa Bay Buccaneers
Washington Redskins

Basketball

National Basketball Association
Atlanta Hawks
Boston Celtics
Chicago Bulls
Cleveland Cavaliers
Dallas Mavericks
Denver Nuggets
Detroit Pistons
Golden State Warriors
Houston Rockets
Indiana Pacers
Los Angeles Clippers
Los Angeles Lakers
Milwaukee Bucks
New Jersey Nets
New York Knickerbockers
Philadelphia 76ers
Phoenix Suns
Portland Trail Blazers
Sacramento Kings
San Antonio Spurs
Seattle SuperSonics
Utah Jazz
Washington Bullets

Hockey

National Hockey League
Boston Bruins
Buffalo Sabres
Calgary Flames
Chicago Black Hawks
Detroit Red Wings
Edmonton Oilers
Hartford Whalers
Los Angeles Kings
Minnesota North Stars
Montreal Canadiens
New Jersey Devils
New York Islanders
New York Rangers
Philadelphia Flyers
Pittsburgh Penguins
Quebec Nordiques
St. Louis Blues
Toronto Maple Leafs
Vancouver Canucks
Washington Capitals
Winnipeg Jets